TROY

AEGEAN
SEA

BES

ATHENS

NAXOS

MILETUS

MILOS

THERA

SEA OF CRETE

RHODES

KNOSSOS

CRETE

C. Kaeser

MYCENAE

MYCENAE
FROM MYTH TO HISTORY

ATHINA
CACOURI

ROBERT
McCABE

A NEW PLAY BY JOHN
GUARE

COMMENTARIES BY LISA **WACE FRENCH**

THE LANDSCAPE BY DANIEL **FALLU**

ABBE VILLE PRESS

For Spyros Iakovidis

pp. 2, 6, 284, and 287

This drawing of a detail of the facade of the Treasury of Atreus was made by the Italian painter Simone Pomardi in 1805, while he was traveling in the Argolid with Edward Dodwell. It is in the collection of the Packard Humanities Institute and we are grateful for permission to use it.

Parking lot at the Citadel in 1954 with the photographer's rented VW beetle in sole occupation. This newly constructed amenity was sited over a flourishing tobacco field, which the well-turned soil from Schliemann's excavations made exceptionally fertile. Such soil from excavation dumps was always sought after for spreading on the fields.

CONTENTS

Robert McCabe in 1955 with Nikolaos Demopoulos, the late father-in-law of Professor Kim Shelton of the
University of California, Berkeley. Mr. Demopoulos, a local farmer, worked at the excavations that summer.
Dr. Shelton has been working at the site since 1989.

ROBERT McCABE

PREFACE

Betrayal. Violence. Revenge. Cannibalism. Fabulous wealth. The legends of the dynasty of Atreus, which ruled Mycenae, make Hollywood pale by comparison. They have inspired literature and art through the ages, from Homer, Aeschylus, Sophocles, and Euripides to Voltaire, Jacques Offenbach, Eugene O'Neill, Jean-Paul Sartre, and Martha Graham.

But until the archaeological excavations carried out by Heinrich Schliemann in 1876, what relation the legends had—if any—to the historical reality and landscape of Greece was completely unknown.

As the crow flies Mycenae lies some fifty-five miles southwest of Athens. Its ruins cover a rocky outcropping nestled between Mounts Prophet Ilias and Zara on the edge of the fertile Argive plain. The site is distinguished by some unique and memorable features: the majestic Lion Gate, a grave circle of huge stone slabs, and massive beehive-vaulted tholos tombs.

Now after over a century of digging and study we can say that for some 400 years, between roughly 1600 and 1200 BC, the city of Mycenae was the center of a flourishing civilization with great military, commercial, and cultural power. Mycenae came to dominate the territory associated with King Minos of Crete, whose navy and trading vessels had once ruled the Aegean. The Mycenaeans wrote the Greek language in a sophisticated syllabic script adapted from the Cretans, and they used it to maintain meticulous records of economic activity. Their painting and metalworking skills were remarkable. Their handsome citadel commanding the Argive plain was given the epithets "well-built" and "rich in gold."

The myths that haunt the site have been a powerful force in stimulating its study. They tell that sometime in the distant past a man named Agamemnon held power in Mycenae. He was ruthless, arrogant, and uncompromising. He cajoled or commanded city-states from across the Hellenic world to prepare their forces for an assault on Troy.

The stated objective was to recover the wife of Agamemnon's brother Menelaus, the beautiful Helen, who had been kidnapped by Paris, prince of Troy. A massive expedition against that Asian power—strategically positioned at the entrance to the Dardanelles—was mounted, involving 1,200 ships and over 100,000 men. The Greeks won the Trojan War after ten long years. But when Agamemnon returned to his palace he was murdered by his wife and her lover. (Agamemnon's son Orestes avenged the murder of his father by killing his mother, but for this act of impiety was pursued by the Furies and went mad.) Instead of enhancing the wealth and power of Mycenae, the victory over Troy seems instead to have been the death knell of the city and civilization.

Excavations confirm that within a generation or so of the period of the Trojan War, Mycenaean civilization had disappeared. Its cities were depopulated, the palaces burnt and destroyed, the writing system lost, the artists gone. Poverty set in.

We may never know exactly what happened around 1200 BC to undermine this powerful site and society. Perhaps, alongside the poets, we may suggest that a decade of war weakened the Mycenaeans' ability to defend themselves internally. The great warriors were away from home and the fighting left their ranks heavily depleted. Perhaps citizens rebelled against the control exercised by the administrators of an absent king. Or the slaves revolted. Earthquakes may have weakened the system, or perhaps it was disease, or climate change. Or a Dorian invasion or migration. Perhaps the so-called Sea Peoples accelerated the demise. Or religious differences. Maybe the region's city-states became locked in internecine wars after their collaboration at Troy. Perhaps the problems started with a disruption of their trading partners and routes. We are learning more every year.

Mycenaean civilization may have disappeared, but memories of a glorious and prosperous lost era had taken root with the poets and singers. The stories of the city's kings and heroes with their gold-studded swords were kept alive and embellished by generations of oral poets. For four hundred years these histories were passed down until, perhaps around 750 BC, a famed bard, a blind man named Homer, is said to have put the stories in more or less the form we know today. They were written down, in the new alphabet that the Greeks had adopted from Phoenicia, as the *Iliad* and the *Odyssey*.

You might think that without the power and beauty and rhythms of Homer's poetry Mycenae would be just another blur in the kaleidoscope of prehistoric cultures of the Balkans and near east. But if you visit the site and then visit the Mycenaean treasure collection in the National Archaeological Museum in Athens you may well agree that there is something about Mycenaean civilization that is unique and intriguing, and makes it worth understanding and probing in more depth.

The goal of the authors is to give the reader a sense of Mycenae as a place, as an archaeological excavation project, and as a civilization that is emerging from prehistory. The foundation of this book was laid sixty years ago during an exhibition at Princeton University about the decipherment of Linear B script that included some of my photographs of Mycenae. Alan Wace dropped in on the exhibition and subsequently invited me to come the following summer and take more photographs of the site. Then the catalyst for the book—the sad catalyst—more than half a century later was the death of our friend Spyros Iakovidis in 2013. He was the last of three great archaeologists who worked at Mycenae whom I knew well and for whom I had developed unbounded respect and admiration—for their knowledge, their intelligence, and their dedication. The others were Alan Wace and George Mylonas.

The text for this volume was written by Athina Cacouri, the renowned and versatile Greek writer of mystery stories, history, and historical novels. Her late husband was Spyros Iakovidis. She has long been an insider in the world of Mycenaean archaeology and she presents the story of the men and women whose passionate devotion to archaeology has brought so much of Greece's shadowy prehistory into history. The Greek artist Titina Chalmatzi has contributed portraits of each of the story's key figures.

The myths surrounding Mycenae, coupled with Homer's epic poems, were an important reason why—even a thousand years later in Classical times—Mycenae was so profoundly embedded in the Hellenic consciousness. The family history is as complicated as it is lurid. We are deeply honored that for this volume the great Irish-American playwright John Guare has written a new play, *War Bride*, which helps to elucidate the twists and turns of the Atreid dynasty. The action takes place on a Mycenaean warship returning from Troy, through a conversation between King Agamemnon and his war prize, the Trojan princess and prophetess Cassandra.

The photographs were taken in 1954 and 1955 using a Rolleiflex with a 75mm f3.5 Zeiss lens and Kodak Plus-X film. The commentaries on these photographs were written by Lisa Wace French, daughter of Alan Wace. They offer a unique insight into life at the excavations and the modern village nearby. Mrs. French prepared the timeline as well. There are few people in the world who come close to her knowledge of and devotion to Mycenaean history.

Aristotle wrote about the effect of climate change on Mycenae in its long-standing rivalry with Argos. From that seed came the idea of including in the book a review of the landscape, geology, and climate of the site, written by Dan Fallu, a Boston University–based geoarchaeologist who works at Mycenae and understands its topography rock by rock.

The Greek edition of this book did not have photographs of the magnificent objects that have been found at Mycenae, since for an Athenian it's a short walk to see the finds at the National Archaeological Museum. For this edition the Museum has very generously made available images of some of these extraordinary treasures, though what you will see here is not even the tip of the iceberg.

As I write this preface in the fall of 2015, the Greek Ministry of Culture has just made a dramatic announcement. Jack Davis and Sharon Stocker of the University of Cincinnati have completed the excavation of one of the richest and most interesting Bronze Age tombs to have been discovered in Greece in a generation. Dating to around 1500 BC, the tomb is located adjacent to the Palace of Nestor in Pylos. It appears to be the tomb of a warrior and contained over a thousand objects, of gold, silver, bronze, or precious stones— including jewelry, cups, seal stones, and weapons. Many appear to be of Cretan origin. The discovery has brought important new information to the quest for understanding Mycenaean civilization.

So the saga continues, with remarkable archaeological finds and painstaking analysis helping to put together pieces of the puzzle of this mysterious and fascinating civilization.

Linear B tablet from Pylos. An 657. The text records deployment orders for defenders of the coastal areas around Pylos. National Archaeological Museum, Athens. E.A. Galanopoulos photo.

MYCENAEAN

1700 BC	1650 BC	1600 BC	1550 BC	1500 BC	1450 BC	1400 BC

Earliest settlement on the site dates as early as 6000 BC

Grave Circle B [burials from 1675 to 1550]

1650 Beginning of Mycenae's rise to power

First palace on summit

Eruption of Thera [between 1628 and 1525]

Grave Circle A [1610–1490] Golden death masks

Strong contacts with Crete

Early trade links to East & West

Tholos and Chamber Tombs both in use

Linear B comes into use at Knossos

Trade expansion to East

Treasury of Atreus built

Strong Mycenaean presence in Knossos

T I M E L I N E

BY LISA WACE FRENCH

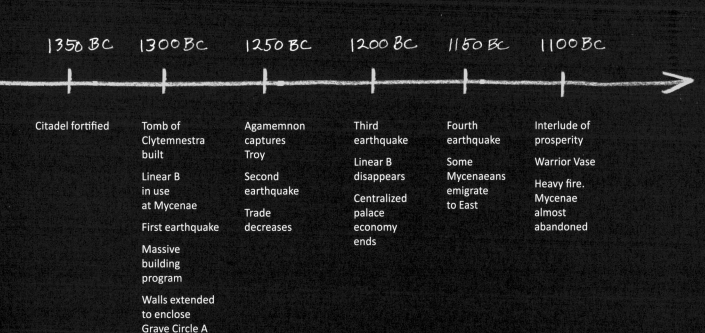

1350 BC	1300 BC	1250 BC	1200 BC	1150 BC	1100 BC
Citadel fortified	Tomb of Clytemnestra built	Agamemnon captures Troy	Third earthquake	Fourth earthquake	Interlude of prosperity
	Linear B in use at Mycenae	Second earthquake	Linear B disappears	Some Mycenaeans emigrate to East	Warrior Vase
	First earthquake	Trade decreases	Centralized palace economy ends		Heavy fire. Mycenae almost abandoned
	Massive building program				
	Walls extended to enclose Grave Circle A				
	Lion Gate built				

ATHINA CACOURI

MYCENAE: FROM MYTH TO HISTORY

S ummer. 1954. It was almost noon when two Americans in their early twenties, the McCabe brothers, were approaching Mycenae. They had been driving for almost four hours from Athens, where they had rented their Volkswagen, a distance that was barely seventy miles, but the roads were narrow—two cars could pass each other only with caution—signs were absent, there were many potholes and as many blind turns, around which they might find themselves face to face with a donkey plodding along under its load of wood with its owner sidesaddle or with the local bus, battered, overflowing with passengers and wobbling beneath the weight of bundles, baskets, suitcases, crates, and live fowl, all piled atop its roof or even a string of four barefoot little girls, holding hands and tugging the family goat with a rope—scenes delightfully exotic for the New Yorkers but which demanded full concentration on the wheel and precluded speeding.

Thus it was nearly noon when the acropolis of Mycenae appeared in the distance, on the edge of the Argive plain. At its peak, the pitiless August glare levelled the volumes and absorbed the colors, leaving only brown and yellow hues. Stones and earth baked in the sun. With their outlines blurred, the ancient walls, the craggy twin-peaked mountain behind them, and, at their feet, the fields cut up into plots by dry-stone walling, became one with the arid landscape.

Suddenly a straight wide road lined with eucalyptus trees opened up to their left. The two brothers followed, thinking it would lead them directly to the famous archaeologi-

The stationmaster Theodosios Papadopoulos relaxes at Mycenae station (at the village of Phychtia on the main road from Corinth). The board shows the timetable of the Up trains to Athens and the Down trains to Kalamata; both the fast *autokinetamaxa* (automotrice) and the slow *atmelatos* (steam trains) are listed. Today there is no train service to Mycenae.

cal site, but after about 550 yards the road narrowed, then squeezed between forlorn little mud-brick houses. Small bunches of tobacco leaves hung drying in some yards—the peasants' scanty efforts to add something to the meager income yielded by a few olive trees or the five or six animals they raised. There was no water-well to be seen at any of the houses. Solitude and quiet prevailed. The old people were dozing in the shade of their houses. Men and women were still out in the fields working alongside their children. An old woman, in the customary black kerchief and dress, came panting down the road, carrying in each hand a pail full of water.

The two brothers were not taken aback by the poverty of this country—they had seen it all over Greece, where they had been travelling for the last month. One of them, Bob, was an amateur photographer and had already recorded dozens of landscapes and views of everyday life.

THE BACKGROUND

It was the hospitality of a Greek fellow student at Princeton University that had brought the McCabes to Greece, along with the glory of Antiquity and perhaps even a faint afterglow of the splendor of 1940. During that bleak winter of World War II, the unbelievable pluck of this small nation in refusing to submit to the Italian colossus attacking it, the unhoped-for victories and the formidable courage it displayed in the mountains of Epirus, had stirred hearts the world over for a moment—one very brief moment. So maybe there is a drop of compassion in McCabe's technique, endowing his pictures with a sensitivity, a psychological attunement, which make them still convey to us today, half a century later, the primeval memories on the face of a peasant, the harmony of antiquated crafts, the joyous vitality of barefoot children, the groan of deeply war-wounded Greece and its heartbeat.

Be that as it may, that August noon the brothers, having found a place to leave their car, entered the fenced-in archaeological site, walked up the slope, and, passing through the Lion Gate, entered the deserted acropolis. Up above they were transfixed by the superb view. The older brother found a low wall to sit on and gazed about, while Bob, thrilled by the landscape, its myth, and the challenge of trying to photograph under this profusion of hard light, readied his camera.

Two years prior, in 1952, the citadel of Mycenae, famous since Antiquity, had made the front pages of Greek newspapers with the spectacular gold finds of a new Grave Circle. And again just a few months earlier, during the fall of 1953, the decipherment of Linear B script was announced to the international scholarly community, which for the last fifty years had been striving—sifting through the plethora of new data brought up by the many excavations, the conflicting theories which were brought forward, and the ancient legends—to find the way to a true reading of Greek prehistory.

In a sense, the efforts of Robert McCabe to capture with his lens, in that blinding midday light of August 1954, the fleeting relief of the fabulous seat of Mycenaean kings finds a distant similarity to the efforts of the archaeologists and scholars to discern, through millennia of hazy legends, the identity of the Mycenaeans and the features of their civilization.

ANTIQUARIANISM AND LOOTING

Homer refers to Mycenae as "rich in gold," but for many centuries one could see only the massive boulders of the walls and the gigantic relief decoration of the Lion Gate. The buildings inside the acropolis—disused, looted, abandoned for centuries—were progressively collapsing, becoming shapeless mounds, rubble, which slowly buried all the remains of ancient human activity. Travelers came from all over the world, looked, and left, to later describe in their books the few things one could see on the surface of the ground. Diodorus of Sicily, Strabo, Pausanias, they all refer to Mycenae. Throughout the seventeenth, eighteenth, and nineteenth centuries the number of travelers increased; dozens

came from various European countries, but none could contribute anything to our knowledge of the acropolis, none until Heinrich Schliemann, the inspired amateur who believed, heart and soul, in the truth of Homer's ancient epic and devoted his life to proving it.

The nineteenth century had just entered its seventh decade and archaeology was still a very young science, with a methodology for excavation taking only its first steps. Archaeology hadn't yet properly differentiated itself from the European interest in the artistic vestiges of Rome and Ancient Greece—the "antiquarianism" which was not so much an attempt to approach the past, but rather a treasure-hunt with the sole aim of retrieving from the earth, or stripping from splendid but inaccessible monuments of Antiquity, ornaments for the homes of the rich and for the collections that European lovers of antiquities had begun to assemble in mansions or museums. In Greece, during the Turkish occupation but also afterwards, people in their general poverty and illiteracy saw in everything ancient a means of making a few pennies, while the prospective buyers, mainly Europeans, ransacked the country without realizing what they were destroying. But there were also others, even rugged warriors of the 1821 War of Independence, who saw their Greek identity and the future of their country as indissociable from the antiquities, and bitterly proclaimed with the war hero Makriyannis: "Those are what we fought for."

Accordingly the Greek State, as soon as it was born, tiny and feeble though it was, took steps to protect its antiquities. In 1829 Governor Kapodistrias, the first Head of State of Greece, founded an Archaeological Service; it was staffed, however, by just one archaeologist, Andreas Moustoxydis, who had one and a half assistants: painter/lithographer Athanasios Iatridis and Archimandrite Leondios Kampanis, who was also the director of the orphanage on Aegina. Fewer than three men, while the antiquities were innumerable.

And how could it have been otherwise, when the very existence of this first Greek State was more than precarious, flanked as it was on one side by its former oppressors, the Ottoman Turks, and on the other by the rapacious and conflicting Great Powers, none of whom believed that the survival of Greece was in their best interest, let alone its expansion. Sad was the series of threats against Greece and the blackmailing practiced by these states who, while sharing amongst themselves the riches of all the world, still stooped to extorting now and again a few thousand pounds from Greece and to abusing her on ridiculous pretexts. However, Greece has forever lived mainly as an idea in the soul of her spiritual children, surviving there and therein reborn.

Such were the Greeks who came at that time to embellish the new State with elegant and beautiful public buildings, to endow it with welfare institutions, and to generously offer their time, taking upon themselves a share of the state's responsibilities. That's how the Archaeological Society at Athens was established in 1837 upon the initiative of a wealthy businessman with a passion for antiquity. Men of letters, politicians, and diplomats supported the venture. The objective was to supplement and assist the State Archaeological Service in the discovery and restoration of antiquities. The resources were limited, the enthusiasm boundless; antiquities were a magnificent but very heavy legacy and extremely costly.

THE ADVENT OF SCHLIEMANN

One of the first sites the Archaeological Society attended to was Mycenae. In 1841 the curator of antiquities at the Central Museum, Kyriakos Pittakis, was sent there. He was an important and loyal servant of antiquities, one who would soon become the soul of monument maintenance on and around the Acropolis of Athens. Pittakis freed the Lion Gate from the soil that obstructed it and made some minor improvements. But things were not endangered at Mycenae, while elsewhere there was an urgent need for emergency interventions. As a result, nothing further was done until 1874 and the advent of Heinrich Schliemann, the already famous excavator of Troy.

Schliemann was a singular person, a German who became a millionaire in order to prove Homer right; who chose for his wife a Greek woman, beautiful but also capable of learning the Homeric poems; who used in his personal correspondence a somewhat idiosyncratic ancient Greek language; and who built in Athens a gorgeous home, full of allusions to ancient Greece, that can still be seen today, since it houses the Numismatic Museum. Schliemann asked the Archaeological Society for permission to dig in Mycenae and of course received it.

View of Grave Circle A and the Great Ramp showing the dromos (entrance passage) of the Tomb of Atreus in the background, with Argos in the distance on the far left.

The village was then called Charvati, but besides its name it must not have differed much from what the McCabe brothers saw some eighty years later, renamed Mycenae. Change in Greece, a country afflicted by so many calamities and deprived of all means to develop, came in very slow stages.

Judging from the condition of the region at the end of the nineteenth century, there was no reason to believe that after all the devastation, pillaging, foreign conquests, barbaric invasions, and general wretchedness prevailing for centuries around the ancient site of the Atreids—the family of Atreus about whom Homer and the tragic poets had sung—one would then find any trace of its ancient civilization and wealth.

Schliemann did not give such doubts a second thought. Working at great speed, he opened some thirty exploratory trenches and almost immediately identified a cemetery, known today as Grave Circle A (to the right as one enters the site through the Lion Gate). He excavated five of the graves, found them undisturbed and full of dazzling grave goods—funeral masks, weapons, jewelry—as well as gold, gold in abundance and beautifully crafted. There, for all to see, was the proof that Mycenae was truly "rich in gold" just as Homer had described!

One of the many feats of this surprising individual, Schliemann, was his proving, once and for all, that in every attempt to reconstruct the past, whether written sources exist or not, it is very unwise to undervalue the importance of myth and tradition.

New confirmation of the wealth of the Mycenaeans came a little later when another archaeologist, Panagiotis Stamatakis, found between two walls, in the remains of an ancient house near the south section of Grave Circle A, a hoard of mixed precious vessels and jewelry. Apparently, with danger approaching, they must have been hidden there by their owners who did not survive to come back and retrieve them.

All these objects were much marveled at, but soon their beauty and superior craftsmanship raised questions: where had those hardened warriors, the Atreids, found all that gold? How had they come to possess it? How were they suddenly capable of so expertly working precious metal and stone? Was it at all plausible that they could have made such a huge cultural leap on their own?

Schliemann had no doubts on the matter: the Mycenaeans were lauded by Homer, and it was the civilization of the Achaeans that his own excavations had brought to light. He even maintained that in one of the gold masks, which he had found in the royal tombs, one could see imprinted the very features of the man who had led the Achaeans to Troy, because this was the funeral mask of Agamemnon himself!

TSOUNTAS

The archaeologist who succeeded Schliemann at Mycenae was an entirely different personality, with a different kind of mind and a different education. Christos Tsountas was born in 1857, that is to say at the time when King Otto and his Queen Amalia ruled Greece, and just a few years after the English and French had once again blockaded the country—this time as a punishment for attempting to get involved in the Crimean War on the side of the Russians against the Ottoman Empire. At that time the frontier of the Greek State extended from Platamon to Arta—thus leaving the birthplace of Tsountas, which was Stenimachos in Eastern Rumelia (today's South Bulgaria), very far within the boundaries of what was then the Ottoman Empire. Tsountas first learned to read and write in Stenimachos and nearby Filippoupolis, which at the time boasted fine schools. However he was sent to Athens to finish secondary school, probably because back then all of Hellenism had its eye on the Greek State and any parents who could, would send their children to Athens "to go to school and become Greeks." He must have been a gifted youth because—as was often the case at the time—a well-to-do uncle later sent him to a university in Germany.

Tsountas enrolled in the School of Civil Engineering at Hanover but soon after moved to Munich, to follow the lectures of Heinrich Brunn. This eminent archaeologist opened new roads in the way monuments and works of art should be examined; he shifted the focus from mainly aesthetic evaluation to dating. One should no longer concentrate on why and how beautiful something was, but instead search for ways to place it in its chronological order, to grasp what the object itself, and whatever surrounded it when it was found, had to say to us about the sequence of events in history.

At the age of twenty-three Tsountas obtained his doctorate. A photo from this period shows him as a young man with a fairly narrow face, straight nose, a thick handlebar moustache, and sparse hair covering a prominent forehead. In another photograph, taken twenty years later, we see that his hair has disappeared, the crown of his head is bare and somewhat pointed, his face has filled in. The first impression is that he is smiling but when you look closely, you notice that his gaze is the same—serious, focused, fixed hard on something only he can see before him. You sense the weight of inner calm, a psychological steadiness, but perhaps also some reticence, maybe coldness. However, the most eminent poet of that time, Kostis Palamas, described him as "unaffected and temperate and lucid and abstemious, and witty too," and maintained that we find him exactly the same in his writings.

Not much is known about Tsountas' private life. He must have had a mild disposition, since we hear nothing of clashes or friction during his solitary life. He entered easily and smoothly into the special professor-student rapport, submitting readily to the authority of those who had something to teach him, while his own students became, in their turn, the leaders of the next generation of Greek archaeologists. He did defend his principles and convictions when necessary, but he did not get embroiled in disputes, especially about politics. Honors and positions of power did not interest him. He earned and maintained the respect of personalities such as the eminent scholar Stefanos Coumanoudis, the satirist Emmanuel Roídis, and the poet Kostis Palamas. His sense of duty must have been extremely strong and unflagging: from the moment he became a university professor—a post into which he was practically forced—he concentrated all his time and energy on the preparation of his courses, sacrificing his work as a field archaeologist, which he adored, and his publications, which were very important.

Having graduated from Munich, this serious young man went back to Stenimachos and for two years taught at the Zographeion College. But Stefanos Coumanoudis had already noticed and appreciated him, and took it upon himself to find a position for the young scholar. The next year Tsountas was appointed ephor in the Greek government's Archaeological Service, and in 1884 he became a member of the Archaeological Society.

Tsountas learned excavation techniques alongside the expert Panagiotis Stamatakis, systematically and silently, just as he carried out everything else assigned to him, which was initially work on archaeological sites of the Classical period. Very soon, though, his interests shifted to prehistory, especially after 1886, when at Coumanoudis' insistence the Archaeological Society assigned him to excavate at Mycenae.

For twelve years Tsountas worked at Mycenae, thus inaugurating the systematic survey and excavation of the site—work which has continued, with very few interruptions, for 130 years. He had his own way of working: he would dig in many different spots and did not publish in minute detail, as would happen today, but instead used the data he gathered to support conclusions leading to a broader picture. His vision was comprehensive and his mind quick at associating and connecting. All subsequent excavators at Mycenae "encountered everywhere before them the traces of the true pioneer and first genuine researcher of a civilization which had only just started to come to light," as described by Spyros Iakovidis, the last Director of Excavations in Mycenae to date. Tsountas' book, *The Mycenaean Age: A study of the monuments and culture of pre-Homeric Greece* (Macmillan, London, 1897), is fundamental.

One of Tsountas' conclusions was that the Mycenaean was the ancestor of the Classical civilization—its very roots an inseparable part of it, and consequently, it would be impossible to "take out of the background of Greek history the wondrous stage settings which throughout Antiquity never ceased to inspire poets and craftsmen." Thus wrote Tsountas in 1897 and no one questioned that the Mycenaeans were indeed the forefathers of Greek civilization. But these Mycenaeans, who were they exactly?

Very little was known at the time about prehistory and even less had been confirmed. Many archaeological sites were still totally unknown. Likewise unknown were entire civilizations—like that of Crete, which started coming to light in 1900, or that of Akrotiri on Thera, talk of which began as mere conjecture two decades later. The technique of excavating—the systems and the tools of the excavator—had just begun to develop and it had not yet been established as a fact that archaeology could, by its own means, grasp the features and the course of a civilization that had not left written accounts of its history—that is a "prehistoric" one, as they called it.

We could visualize the period from the nineteenth century until the first fifty years of the twentieth century as a landscape initially pitch-dark, which received successive shafts of light here and there, suddenly and haphazardly. Mycenae, Knossos, Pylos . . . it was these small, illuminated areas that the great archaeologists of the time attempted to connect with each other. With admirable stretching of their imaginations, and inevitably with a certain arbitrariness, they erected bridges over the large, dark chasms. It was a time of bold ideas and impressive discoveries.

The culminating point came in the middle of the 1950s, precisely when Bob McCabe took his pictures at Mycenae. But the main controversy, the one that revolved around the two poles of Mycenae and Knossos, had begun in 1900 with the sensational discoveries of Sir Arthur Evans at Knossos.

The problem was already obvious. Scholars more or less agreed on the time frame of a period, which they called Middle Helladic, from which they were finding the traces of a civilization generally homogeneous, rather poor, low-grade, and definitely Greek throughout the country. But immediately afterwards, abruptly, followed the massive walls of the Mycenaean citadels and the beehive tombs—that is to say great architectural achievements. Meanwhile excavations were steadily bringing to light elegant objects like the two beautiful gold cups Tsountas had discovered at Vapheio, near Sparta. And in Cephalonia, Volos, Aegina, Euboea, and the Aegean islands, but also sporadically on the shores of Asia Minor, the coast of Macedonia, and the Black Sea, Cyprus, and Egypt, in settlements and in tombs, objects were being found that resembled each other and stood out from older ones, as well as from most of those surrounding them—fabulous earthenware vessels, masterpieces of decoration, metalwork, and painting.

Amidst all these outstanding finds there were also some *pithoi*, large earthenware containers that had been found by a talented lover of antiquities, the Cretan Minos Kalokairinos. In 1878, around the same time that Schliemann was working in Mycenae, Kalokairinos dug in an area close to Heraklion, on a hill called Cephala, where he discovered a whole depository with similar ancient *pithoi*. With Crete still under Turkish occupation he decided not to proceed any further because he knew that his finds, should they prove to be valuable, would be shipped off to Constantinople and end up in the museum that the Ottoman State was building. He postponed further work in the belief that Crete would soon be liberated. The location, however, was staked out as important and it was chosen by Evans when he reached the Great Island shortly before 1896, when Crete was granted self-rule.

EVANS

Evans was a famous man and thus we know almost everything about his life. He did not belong, like Tsountas, to a very old civilization, broken up and surviving in scattered fragments, but to the young British Empire, on whose vast territories "the sun never set." Britain was the wealthiest state in the world at the time, mighty and at the vanguard of civilization. His father, Sir John Evans, was a renowned geologist and archaeologist, an individual who had operated a large paper mill, had written serious studies on coins and ancient stone tools, had been awarded honorary doctorate degrees from distinguished universities, and had served on a number of boards of prominent scientific societies, such as the Antiquaries and the British Museum—in other words, he was a man of many talents, very learned, wealthy, and with a brilliant position in society.

Arthur, his firstborn son, naturally received a first-rate education, went to Oxford and Göttingen, and at a young age was appointed keeper at the Ashmolean Museum at Oxford. At the start he worked on ethnography and archaeology in the Balkan states, but in 1893 he went to Crete. He was forty years old. However, fate had not left him unscathed—he had recently lost his wife. He mourned for her for the rest of his years.

SIR ARTHUR JOHN EVANS

In any case, the reason he went to Crete was because he had observed that some seal stones in the Ashmolean collection bore incised signs and believed that the latter represented some kind of script. All the seal stones of this type came from Crete and so he went there in the hope of finding more. He looked at a number of locations and chose the one discovered by Kalokairinos. He bought the land—as we said he was very wealthy—and began his excavation.

From the start it was clear that he had stumbled upon an intricate palatial complex. In the decades that followed, Evans uncovered the extraordinary labyrinthine palace of Knossos and an entire civilization, which he called Minoan.

With all his erudition, and the exceptional capacity of his rare mind for associating and combining, he dedicated himself to research on Minoan civilization and the impact it had on the surrounding areas—the Aegean, eastern Mediterranean, and mainland Greece.

His work both as an excavator and as a writer is monumental. He was not infallible. But he respected truth and strove to discern it. It was he who drew out of the "long night of human oblivion" the centuries of Minoan magnificence.

THE PALACE AT KNOSSOS

From the very first years of the excavation it became apparent that a highly sophisticated civilization had gradually developed on Crete. The architecture of the palace, the amenities it provided, the beautiful wall-paintings, the luxurious vessels, even the earthenware for everyday use, spoke of a society that was stratified, affluent, and refined. Taken together with finds from many other sites, both on the island and elsewhere, they showed that Crete had been the seat of a great maritime and commercial power which had dominated the Aegean since the seventeenth century BC, and which had developed dynamic contacts, both commercial and cultural, with the coasts of Asia Minor and Egypt.

Many of Evans' finds showed direct affinity to these objects—precious and of a refined taste—that were being discovered in Mycenaean acropolises and graves all over mainland Greece. Thus, in his mind, the idea emerged that the Mycenaean civilization was born out of the Minoan.

The west side of Grave Circle A with Mount Zara in the background. Morning light.

As for the little signs on the seal stones that originally brought Evans to Crete, after the first strikes of the pick in 1900 at Knossos he found hundreds of clay tablets neatly piled, baked by the conflagration that had destroyed the Palace. The tablets were either in the shape of the pages of a book or in the shape of a palm-leaf and bore the signs of a script similar to those on the seal stones.

Soon Evans identified three writing systems: one system consisted of stylized representations of objects. It was the oldest and he called it hieroglyphics. The other two featured simple, linear shapes: curves and straight lines. He identified two different sets, which despite their resemblance displayed very significant differences. The older one he called Linear A script, while the more recent one he called Linear B.

What could have been the use of these ancient tablets? It was easy to recognize many ideograms as utensils or animals; it was also easy to recognize numbers, decades, hundreds, thousands. Thus, one easily came to the conclusion that this was an archive, the Royal General Accounting Office of the Minoan State, so to say.

Although the language was unknown and therefore the words could not be understood, here was an overwhelming element of superiority of the Minoans over the Mycenaeans—or so it seemed. A thousand years before the Greeks adapted the Phoenician script to their language, the Minoans knew how to write theirs! It would be a great stroke of luck if a bilingual tablet were found, facilitating the decipherment of the tablets and determining the language of the Minoans. But even without it, Evans was optimistic that he would be able to decipher the script himself. Out of the approximately three thousand tablets Evans found, he published only fourteen in 1909 and another 120 in 1935; and he was very angry indeed when a further thirty-nine circulated without his approval.

The Knossos tablets provoked the interest of many scholars and learned men all over the world, and a good number set themselves to the task of deciphering them. For Evans himself, these tablets became one of the strongest points—but not the only one, of course—in favor of his theory, a theory advanced to give meaning to the huge volume of data he was producing in Crete, along with many other excavators and scholars all over the Aegean, and beyond. The main objective was to elucidate the nature of Minoan civilization, its range of influence, and its course—and thus answer the question: what happened in the period between the peak of Minoan power in the seventeenth century BC and the thirteenth century BC, when Minoan civilization had declined and the Mycenaean prevailed?

EVANS' THEORY

Evans developed a theory, which was summarized in the 1970s by one of his distinguished successors, Nikolaos Platon, as follows:

> Mycenaean civilization appeared suddenly in Minoan garb. Life changed suddenly and the standard of civilization reached the level which we see in Crete circa 1600 BC (towards the end of the Neopalatial Phase). The population, previously farmers and cattle-breeders, became townspeople, craftsmen, merchants, seamen. They lived with the amenities that had already been developed in Crete. Both men and women donned Minoan dress, their ornaments followed Minoan fashions and on the whole, they adopted a lifestyle which was already centuries-old on Crete. Religion (always according to this theory) acquired a Minoan character and used similar symbols and sacred utensils. Their weapons and their tools became Cretan, and their artistic production and craftsmanship became almost identical to that of Crete. Even the burial customs changed and bring to mind the Cretan view of the afterlife. The deposition of rich grave goods to accompany the dead was established and became widespread. All this impressive "Minoanization" appeared

suddenly, at exactly the period when the new palaces and settlements on Crete suffered extensive destruction, at about the same time when Minoan settlements on the Aegean islands were rebuilt or new ones were established as colonies. This sudden Minoanization (according to Evans), could only be interpreted as the result of the Minoans colonizing far-flung strategic locations in Greek territories. Evans drew a parallel between this colonial advance of the Minoans and the expansion of ancient Greek civilization with its establishment of colonies in broader geographical zones in Asia Minor, the coast of Macedonia, Thrace, and the Black Sea, and in Sicily and Southern Italy. He did admit though that the local Helladic element—basically Greek—had gone on living as a separate entity alongside the Minoan colonists; that it had initially received the Minoans without opposition, enjoying the benefits of their higher civilization; and that it woke up and reacted only at a more advanced stage, when it had already assimilated the fertile teachings of Minoan civilization. Then the Minoan dynasties were overthrown and the local Achaean dynasties were established. Evans insisted that the history of this development was evident in Greek tradition and the Homeric epics. In his opinion, the appearance of a warrior ethos from earliest Mycenaean times, the development of military equipment, and the elaborate fortifications could all be explained by the dangers the foreign Minoan dynasties were facing. Evans was not uncompromising as regards the Helladic influence on Minoan civilization during the Mycenaean period and even earlier. He actually attributed the creation of the "Palace style", during the last phase of the Knossos Palace, to such influences. (Platon, *The History of the Greek Nation*, vol. I, Athens, 1970, p. 242.)

So this is how Evans viewed the historical development and this was the theory he upheld in his public announcements and studies, and of course in his many lectures before always crowded audiences. In 1936, while Hitler was preparing his war and England still hoped to avoid it, Evans offered the Knossos area and Villa Ariadne, the beautiful house he had built there, to the British School at Athens. At the same time he took part in a big exhibition in London at Burlington House commemorating the fiftieth anniversary of the

MICHAEL VENTRIS

founding of the British School of Archaeology at Athens. There Evans, along with other specialists, gave lectures and guided visitors around himself, leaning on his cane—he was pushing eighty at the time and had problems seeing at night. Among the visitors that evening was an inquisitive fourteen-year-old boy who asked persistently if the Linear B script had been deciphered yet. It is highly unlikely that Sir Arthur took much notice.

ENTER MICHAEL VENTRIS

The young boy, whose name was Michael Ventris and who had a rare aptitude for languages, decided—secretly and on the spot—that he would be the one to solve this riddle! He returned to boarding school and devoted all his free time—even at night, with a flash-

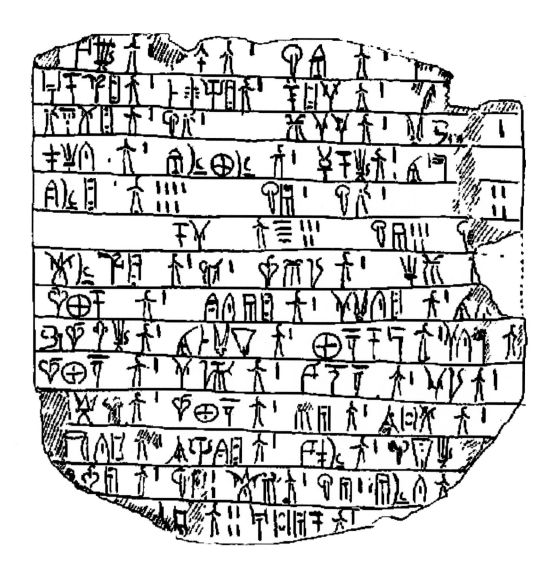

This tablet inscribed in Linear B, Knossos 639, was found during Arthur Evans' 1901–1904 excavations. It was among the limited number of tablets published by Evans in 1909 in Volume 1 of *Scripta Minoa*. Evans conjectured that the tablet presented a list of women's names. He was correct, but until Ventris the names could not be read. Among the ladies are Kopi, Tuzo, Anuwato, Dusani, Pirakara, Kepu, and Warati. The sons and daughters ("kowo" and "kowa") of some of the women are noted as well. (With thanks to Dr. John Younger.)

light under the blankets—to studying everything that had been written about Linear B. His grades in the classes he took, including Ancient Greek and Latin, were not particularly impressive, and although he got involved with other pursuits throughout his life, he never forgot his vow to solve the riddle of Linear B.

So, after Schliemann, Tsountas, Evans, and Wace—about whom we will talk a little later—Ventris is the fifth protagonist in this story, although perhaps it would be fairer to think of him as the sixth, and to grant fifth place to Alice Kober.

But let's go back to Evans. In 1939 a new triumph awaited him—at least that is how he perceived it at the time. While digging the Mycenaean palace at Pylos, the Greek archaeologist Konstantinos Kourouniotis and the American archaeologist Carl Blegen came upon the buried remains of the palace archives. Hundreds and hundreds of new tablets were thus added to the already known tablets of Knossos. The first reaction was, "Oh! So the keeping of archives was not a Minoan monopoly after all! The Mycenaeans had the same system." This weakened Evans' position somewhat. But immediately afterward it was observed that the script bore an astonishing resemblance to the Linear B script of Crete. Evans concluded that this proved that the Minoan language had spread to mainland Greece, providing further unshakeable proof that the prevailing people were the Minoans, that the kings who resided in the Mycenaean acropolises belonged to Minoan dynasties, and that they had brought their language along with them.

This led to other conclusions, such as that these foreign rulers had been forced to build the Cyclopean walls in order to protect themselves against the populations they had conquered, and that the end of Mycenaean civilization came when the native people were able to rise up and chase away the alien potentates.

However such theories, based on the opinions of Evans, were not universally accepted. Other, different ones were developing concurrently; the main exponent of them was another Englishman, Alan John Bayard Wace.

A Cambridge graduate, Alan Wace was appointed director of the British School at Athens in 1914 at the age of thirty-five. He held that position, with all that it implied, during the ten very troubled years of World War I, followed by the bitter internal strife between Venizelists and Royalists, one more blockade by the Anglo-French fleets, and with starvation rampant in the capital.

At any rate, in 1920 Wace was granted permission to excavate "temporarily" in Mycenae, which he did with long interruptions until his death in Athens in 1957. He completed, in part, the excavations undertaken by Schliemann and Tsountas; he elucidated, in part, the topography inside the acropolis; he determined the location of the palace and brought to light the grand staircase and the Cult Center; and he excavated new graves outside the walls, as well as many other sites in the surrounding area. Although he also worked elsewhere in Greece, Mycenae and the Mycenaean civilization were his main interests and it was on that subject that he developed his clear thinking and his talent for synthesis, whereas his spiritual approach to Greece is reflected in his book *Greece Untrodden* (1964)—a collection of remarkably well-written short stories—where myth is woven into contemporary life in a Greek countryside as conceived in his imagination.

Wace interpreted the archaeological evidence in a different manner than Evans. His views were again summarized by Nikolaos Platon, in the 1970s, more or less as follows:

Wace admitted that the Middle Helladic world had been Minoanized to a great extent. He emphasized though that basically the character under the new dress remained essentially Helladic. It was born of the same factors that had developed the Middle Helladic civilization, factors very different than the Minoan. Its main trait was the organizing spirit—the thought process that had attained a higher level of logic and aimed at imposing the laws of inner truth on all creation. It was precisely these

ALAN WACE

laws that the later Greeks were to apply, on a larger scale, during the Geometric, the Archaic, and the Classical periods. The Achaeans received the foreign elements and—after a period of dynamic interplay—they assimilated and made them their own, in the same way that later they received and assimilated elements coming from the East in the Archaic period. Their character was combative, hence the heroic spirit expressed in the Homeric poems. They faithfully imitated Minoan art but otherwise they followed their inclination for the organized and the abstract. They preferred the laws of symmetry and harmony to pure naturalism. They adored their weapons and enjoyed them as no other people ever; arms practice was their sport.

So, although abundant Minoan elements had been inherited, a new style was created in every field of art, as a result of these laws of internal truth. The Mycenaeans adopted many aspects of the sophisticated character of Minoan lifestyle, but they basically preserved an austerity of a different tenor, in which the manly and competitive elements were very explicit. They were obviously inclined towards monumental sculpture. And their religion, like that of the Minoans, was inclined towards an anthropomorphic pantheon. (Platon, *The History of the Greek Nation*, vol. I, p. 245.)

MINOANS VERSUS MYCENAEANS

In 1936 young Ventris had set his sights on decoding the tablets he saw at Burlington House, a goal shared by many other scholars and laymen the world over—one of them being the Hellenist Alice Kober. Three years later, in 1939, Kourouniotis and Blegen were bringing to light the fabulously rich archives of the Palace of Pylos with hundreds of tablets. At that point in time the positions of the two opposing camps were very, *very* roughly as follows:

According to Evans and his followers:

The Minoans had colonized mainland Greece. When the native populations began to rise up against them and threaten them, they built the massive walls of the acropolises—which means that Agamemnon and Nestor were Minoans and that all of Greek civilization to come— Geometric, Archaic, and Classical—had its roots in the Minoan. The end of the Mycenaean civilization was a result of internal turmoil, leading to the violent overthrow of the Cretan dynasties that had governed Greece from the seventeenth to the twelfth century BC.

The Lion Gate. This imposing entry to the Citadel was built at the time of Mycenae's greatest expansion when the Citadel Wall was extended westward to encompass the shaft graves of Grave Circle A. The relief is one of the earliest examples of monumental sculpture in Europe. After the time of Pausanias, the gate and the surrounding walls became covered by debris from the slopes above. It was rediscovered by the Venetian architect Francesco Vandeyk in 1700 and gradually cleared, as the many drawings by early nineteenth century visitors attest.

But according to Wace and his followers:

The Mycenaeans, carriers of the earlier Middle Helladic civilization, may have donned Minoan garb—that is to say they copied, imitated, and profited from many external traits of the far superior Minoan civilization, but they preserved unaltered those characteristics of their own, i.e. a competitive and organizing spirit, abstract thinking, and devotion to order and harmony, that would engender the successive phases, the Geometric and the Archaic and finally, the culmination, Classical Greek civilization.

The outbreak of World War II found Evans' side in a slightly advantageous position since the tablets, which had just been discovered at Pylos, demonstrated (as it was thought then) that the Cretans and the Mycenaeans spoke the same language. At this point, research came to a stop, like every other activity that was not related to the war effort.

In the last months preceding the outbreak of the war one of Wace's students, who would later become a distinguished archaeologist, Vronwy Hankey, took part in British excavations in Greece. She recalled:

In those days the argument maintained by Alan Wace and Carl Blegen versus Arthur Evans (seconded by Pendlebury) over Minoan relations with Mycenae seemed to a green student (who never met Evans) to combine an academic sporting event with a serious debate. Carl Blegen, a patient and eloquent teacher, scored for Mycenae when in April 1939 he showed me Nestor's archive at Pylos as it was being excavated. The excavators naturally referred to the spread of tablets as Nestor's speeches.

Vronwy Hankey had already visited Mycenae. There, she writes, the team of archaeologists lived in the only inn of the village, the Belle Helene:

The dig party walked to and from the dig on most days (occasional motorized visitors were very welcome). Helen dropped off at Atreus to supervise the trenches dug north and south of the dromos walls to discover their date. Frank went on up to the citadel summit where the ivory group was found. My patch was west of the Lion Gate. Fifteen graves from MH to LH II showed that the Grave Circle was part of a large cemetery cut in two and built over by the later Cyclopean fortification walls. Lisa made remarkable finds in Schliemann's dump. We ate breakfast in the shade of the Lion Gate, impossible to imagine today, and waged war to protect the cherry jam from raids by large cataglyph ants. Lunch was spread on the slope in the narrow shade outside the Postern Gate. Usually it was chicken stew brought up by Agamemnon, the lame brother of the foreman Orestes. Agamemnon rode regularly to Argos for fresh supplies, and returned with bunches of birds slung in squawking protest from his saddle. 1939 was a nervous summer so visitors to Mycenae were rare…. The heat was tremendous, relieved by one monster thunderstorm, when we stood outside soaking in the delicious cool rain. This was truly a happy summer for Alan, and we celebrated his sixtieth birthday with a midday feast in the Treasury of Atreus, with distinguished guests and friends from Athens, including Professors C. Blegen, B. Hill, G. Karo, Courouniotis, and Sp. Marinatos (who had given me my permit to study in the Museum at Khalkis). We were photographed ranged across the entrance to the tomb chamber, where afterwards some of us sang folk-songs and rounds. This was interesting. If the singers stood in a circle about two meters from the center, their voices returned immediately, giving a feeling that the sounds had never left the mouth. Move a short distance from the center, and the sounds came back in normal resonance. Wulf Schäfer, a German architect based at the American School, who came to help in surveying, became more and more gloomy as the days passed, until towards the end of August he and his shepherd dog left to answer call-up orders. We helped to celebrate the christening of a daughter of the house at the Belle Helene, and a few days later we said goodbye, and left for Nauplion and the hotel with vine-covered restaurant near the quay. The finds were packed away at the Museum, and we returned to Athens. War had been declared against Germany and we all knew that archaeology was over for the duration.

Blegen had of course given the tablets he found at Pylos to the Greek Archaeological Service to clean and photograph. He managed to have the prints sent to him in America and subsequently delivered them to his student Emmett L. Bennett. But when the United States entered the war, Bennett was drafted into the army. In 1941 Evans died. And Michael Ventris, the young boy who had asked the questions about Linear B at the exhibition in Burlington House, enlisted in the Air Force. He was trained as a navigator on bombers and he served in this capacity until the end of the war.

It was subsequently rumored that he had been a secret agent and been trained as a decoder. This would have been very natural. His ancestors on his father's side were military men and had faithfully served the British Empire in the Far East and the Middle East. So from this point of view the young man, a student of architecture at the time, would have been considered a person of trust. But there was also his mother's side.

She was Dora, a beautiful Polish woman, daughter of a rich landowner, who had immigrated to England. Ventris married her in 1920 and they had one son. Very soon after, father Ventris contracted tuberculosis and was forced into early retirement from the Army, while little Michael was diagnosed with chronic bronchial asthma. Dora was affluent, so the couple settled in Switzerland, at Gstaad, on account of its supposedly salutary climate. The young boy was enrolled at the local school, where classes were in French and German. He learned both these languages without any difficulty—at eight he was passionately reading *The Hieroglyphics* by Adolf Erman, in German. He also learned the local dialect, a mixture of Swiss and German, while he continued speaking with his mother in Polish.

When the couple returned to England in 1931 their marriage was falling apart, and in 1935 they divorced. The young boy won a scholarship and went to a boarding school, where he learned Ancient Greek and Latin with the same fluency he had learned the other languages. During vacations he stayed with his mother in various luxury seaside hotels, and after 1935 in an apartment building of a very avant-garde architectural design. Dora lived a life of luxury and associated mostly with artists. In 1938 Ventris senior died.

In 1939, under the Ribbentrop-Molotov Pact, Poland was partitioned between Nazi Germany and Soviet Russia. Dora's property in Poland stopped yielding any income. Suddenly, poverty struck. In 1940 her father died and she herself fell into a deep depression and died soon thereafter from an overdose of barbiturates. Michael stopped referring to her—he appeared cheerful and active on the outside, a young man very sought-after in company, but inside he was tortured by doubts about his worth and the meaning of his life. Nevertheless, he married and decided to study architecture. At the same time he set himself to learn Russian—for no apparent reason at all other than having met the distinguished Russian Constructivist sculptor Naum Gabo, who had taken him under his wing.

In 1942 then, when the army got him, before he even had time to finish his studies, it was perhaps not the proverbial stupidity of the military that left his talent for languages unexploited, but the uneasiness which the military leadership felt about the psychological instability he inherited from his mother's side. Be that as it may, the fact remains that England did not use Michael Ventris in positions of trust either during the war, or even in the beginning of the Cold War, when he continued to serve and also to study the Russian language in more depth.

Michael Ventris seems to have lived his life in a tormentingly fluid environment—place of residence, parent relationships, financial condition, social framework. All seem elusive, all changing from one moment to the next, depriving him of the certitude of predictability. After the war things seem to have entered a different phase. He finished his studies *cum laude* and began working as an architect. Together with his wife they built a house, exactly

as they wanted it, and it was so pioneering in design that it became famous. They had two children. At the same time Michael continued his attempts to decipher Linear B. One could say that through all the blind twists and turns of his life, this was his own Ariadne's Thread.

ALICE KOBER AND HER GRIDS

Many had already puzzled over this unknown script. Evans, although working with the thousands of tablets he had discovered at the Knossos palace, had not managed to advance. Wace, with the few tablets available on the eve of the Second World War, had also tried his hand, but made no progress. Many other archaeologists and philologists in various countries had set themselves the task of unravelling the mystery of the two linear scripts—among them John Chadwick, Emmett L. Bennett, and Alice Kober, whom we have already mentioned.

Alice, born in 1906 in New York, was the daughter of poor Hungarian immigrants. She had swept up scholarships and prizes and became a professor of Latin at Brooklyn College at a very young age. In 1930 she embarked on solving the riddle of Linear B.

A lonely person all her life, Alice does not seem to have been interested in either material comforts or social relations. She lived with her widowed mother and worked from day to night and then some. In one of her last photographs we see her sitting in an armchair; she's rather heavy-set, has a rich head of hair, a square face with large eyes, strong nose, and seemingly tightened lips; her head is turned to the right; she is looking at something in the distance and lower down; her hands lie on an open book and she is holding a pencil in one hand. The lit cigarette which was always next to her is nowhere to be seen.

Kober's mind was exceptional, her will ferocious, and even more ferocious were her appetite and capacity for work. Apart from her native tongue and English, she had already learned—classical philologist that she was—Ancient Greek and Latin; now, to solve the riddle of Linear B, she learned Hittite, Ancient Irish, Akkadian, Sumerian, old Persian, Basque, and Chinese, while for three years she visited Yale, commuting from New York to New Haven daily by train, in order to perfect her Sanskrit. She needed all these languages because the Minoan language was unknown and the key to its identification might lie in any one of the ancient languages.

pp. 50–51
Alan Wace looking out across the Citadel Wall toward the merchants' houses and the terrain to the northwest from the surround wall of Grave Circle A. This is the Grave Circle discovered by Schliemann and from which the fabulous gold objects form a prime display in the National Archaeological Museum in Athens. The discovery in 1951 of a second Grave Circle slightly earlier in date has required the two circles to be distinguished by the addition of the letters A and B to the titles by which they are known.

Her personality seems to us rigid and cold, until we learn that on her own initiative, without prompting from anyone, she learned the Braille system, then transcribed textbooks for her blind students and corrected their written exams—acts of generosity which add an unexpected sweetness to the physiognomy of Kober.

Without abandoning for a single hour her teaching obligations at Brooklyn College, Kober continued struggling with Linear B, at home at night, with her eternal cigarette next to her. In fifteen years of work she filled forty notebooks with comments, deductions, thoughts, remarks, and—following a system of her own invention for the compilation of statistics—she ended up with some 180,000 punch cards.

An additional difficulty for Kober, and for all the other scholars as well, was that the published tablets amounted to no more than a hundred and seventy-two. But in 1946, Kober received a fellowship from the Guggenheim Foundation and was able to travel to Crete, as well as to Oxford, where, with the help of Professor John Linton Myres, a Hellenist very devoted to Evans' memory, she gained access to the Knossos tablets. Photographing them was out of the question in that day and age so during the winter of 1947 she sat down and copied them by hand, one by one.

MORE ABOUT THE RIDDLE

Linear B script is syllabic. That can be easily deduced, because there are only three writing systems in existence: one uses ideograms, that is every object or concept is represented by a symbol—so one necessarily needs thousands of such symbols. A second system uses one symbol for every sound, like modern alphabets, so that approximately thirty different symbols are enough. A third system uses one symbol for every syllable (i.e. two sounds, a consonant and a vowel usually), so that the symbols required are approximately eighty. Evans had from the very start identified almost eighty symbols, both in Linear A and in Linear B; but although both scripts were apparently syllabic, only

Linear B was provided with endings that changed according to the gender of the subject, and whether it was singular or plural, so Linear B was a language that could be declined, while Linear A was not.

So far so good, but it was not enough. Linear B was still an unknown script of an unknown language. How can one then attempt to read such texts? This is what Kober wonders about at the beginning of her article, published in 1945. And she answers: "The first step is to establish beyond any doubt, actual facts as they emerge from the examination of the available texts.… The second step towards the decipherment is to find out, after careful analysis and disciplined reasoning, what conclusions can be drawn on the basis of these facts."

This is what she had done with her punch cards and her attempt to organize in columns and lines the various sounds and their repetitions. Kober made a huge step forward when she distinguished what she called "the triplex." She identified groups of syllables—words—that appeared in three different forms. The first two had the same initial group of characters—that is the same stem—but two different kinds of endings, identical in all the words. In the third form though, the stem appeared shorter by one sign and the ending differed from word to word. She continued her reasoning, reinforcing her arguments with tables. She concluded that the language represented here was truly declined (i.e. that it used genders and cases and verbs that could be declined), and that it followed the rules of the Indo-European languages.

She published her conclusions with a great deal of hesitation in a series of three articles, in 1945, 1946, and 1948, and started laying out 'grids'—that is, parallel horizontal lines intersected by vertical, parallel lines—and placing the extant syllables inside these boxes, in an attempt to classify them, after which she could start looking for their correlation with actual sounds.

Time did not allow for it. In 1950 this gifted woman with her prodigious mind, her unbending will but also a heart that was surely tender, fell ill and died alone, just as she had lived all of her solitary life. Early in 1950 she was already sick and had not replied to the questionnaire she had received from Ventris, as had eleven other distinguished scholars working on Linear B: another American, two Germans, two Italians, one Czechoslovakian, an Austrian, a Bulgarian, a Finn, an Englishman, and a Greek.

THE SOLUTION TO THE RIDDLE

Ventris' aim, when he sent out this questionnaire, was to collect the views of all the serious scholars in the field, and thus make known to all how far each of them had gone and towards which direction. After studying the replies he received, he composed the "Mid-Century Report" and sent it out to all of them. The conclusion was that no progress had been made in the identification of the language! Some believed that it was Hittite, while others were more inclined towards Etruscan.

However, Ventris had been impressed by Kober's disciplined analysis, leading towards firm conclusions regardless of how the elements were pronounced. He worked on the grids which Kober had only sketchily used, developed them into a tool of greater precision, and continued on the same lines.

The following year, in 1951, E. L. Bennett published two articles, "The Pylos tablets transcribed" and "Statistical Notes on the sign-groups from Pylos," studies in which he had been helped by Alice Kober. Now, thanks to these two articles, the material available to scholars reached eight hundred tablets. And a few months later, in February 1952, the 3,000 tablets of Knossos were finally published. All of a sudden, the database was broadened and research progressed with new vigor, facilitated by the multitude of comparisons and combinations that were now finally possible.

Regularly, from January 1951 until June 1952, Ventris sent a "Work Notes" bulletin to the other scholars, in which he described the progress of his work and asked them for comments and observations. To the very end, he believed that the language was Etruscan, while at the same time he was working with conjectures leading to the identification of sounds.

It was a very lucky moment then when he remembered that Kober had identified some words in the Knossos tablets that were not found amongst those from Pylos, and furthermore she had even made a note to the effect that they were probably place-names. Because place-names remain unchanged for long periods of time, Ventris decided to test his findings on some of them.

With the first word he tried, he got A-mi-ni-sos. The harbor of Knossos! The next came up as Ko-no-so. And then something that could be kore, then kouros…. koriandros…. He found endings in –eus/eos…. Greek! *Greek?*

Astounded, he phoned Emmett Bennett: *Could it be Greek?* But this sounded very improbable to Bennett. Ventris too was in a state of shocked disbelief. So deeply rooted in his mind was Evans' theory that the Cretans of King Minos had occupied mainland Greece and introduced their language that the "Work Note" he sent out on the twentieth of June 1952 ends with: "I suspect that if we follow in this direction, the decipherment will sooner or later reach a dead end and would then dissolve into incoherency."

GREEK! IT IS GREEK!

However he persevered, and lo and behold he identified the words *ποιμήν* (shepherd), *κεραμεύς* (potter), *χρυσουργός* (goldsmith), and *χαλκεύς* (coppersmith)! He was also able to make sense of eight sentences! Greek. There was no doubt anymore. The language was Greek! The last "Work Note" had barely reached the recipients when Ventris gave an interview to the BBC Third Programme (July 1, 1952). What he said then can be heard today on YouTube. He mentions very specifically that he managed to read—names, male and female, of professions, of animals, of produce, and phrases. These, he maintains, confirm the conjecture that it has to do with pedestrian written records of the economic transactions of the palace. He also says that on the tablets discovered in Crete he found many Greek words, and even more on the Pylos tablets; that very probably even the Minoans themselves used Greek—this he says will be confirmed when the reading of the tablets is completed. He also touches on the great controversy regarding the sequence and the relations between the two civilizations, the Minoan and the Mycenaean. He concludes that there is still a lot of work to be done before there is universal agreement among scholars about the solution to the problem.

This announcement went almost unnoticed by the scholarly world! But John Chadwick heard it. The war found Chadwick a freshman at Cambridge. He had enlisted in the Navy, but the Secret Service pulled him out, gave him some basic training, dispatched him to Cairo, and set him to decoding the less important messages of the Italian navy. He was so successful in this job that they took him to work at the famous Bletchley Park, where he learned Japanese and was soon monitoring Japanese agents in Bern and Stockholm. In 1945 he was demobilized and went back to Cambridge to complete his studies. There he worked for a time with some of his fellow students on Linear B, applying the deciphering methods he had been taught in the army. They already knew of Ventris' work but since the published material was still very limited, they lost heart and stopped working on the problem.

Chadwick developed into a good Hellenist. He specialized in ancient Greek dialects and formed original views on the way the Mycenaeans must have pronounced the Greek language. On that famous day, the first of July 1952, Chadwick, upon hearing Ventris, realized that the latter's claims were compatible with his own ideas. Especially in the word *χρυσο Fοργός* mentioned by Ventris—which was exactly as he expected it to be. Encouraged by that, he went and found John Myers at Oxford, who in turn showed him what Ventris had sent him.

Chadwick was convinced that the path Ventris was following was the right one and he offered to collaborate as "a mere Hellenist." Ventris promptly accepted because he knew that his own knowledge of Greek would not be sufficient to fully work things out. So they worked together until Ventris' death in 1956—a tragic death because it is not at all certain whether his car crashed into a parked truck because of the darkness of the night, or whether it was a deliberate exit from life, similar to his mother's. A death doubly tragic because it happened only four years after the BBC interview which scholars had received so coolly. Most remained unconvinced that Linear B had been deciphered and that the language of Linear B was Greek. This had perhaps fed the doubts that tormented Ventris as to whether or not he was a genius and whether or not his life was worth living.

These doubts were of course morbid, because already in 1953 the two men had prepared an article entitled "Evidence for the Greek Dialect in the Mycenaean Archives," and they had submitted it to Carl Blegen. That distinguished excavator of Pylos had studied it and agreed with their conclusions; subsequently the article was accepted and published in the prestigious *Journal of Hellenic Studies* in 1953. Then the news spread quickly in the scholarly community, and with tremendous impact.

Of course many archaeologists and scholars were still cautious. Evans' shadow weighed heavily. And it was difficult to accept that the sophisticated Minoans had been conquered by the coarse Achaeans, and that Crete had not colonized mainland Greece but the other way around: the Mycenaeans had settled in the palace where King Minos had once ruled. But evidently many links were still missing before the when and the how of this reversal could be proven. Even twenty years later not all the historians and archaeologists had been convinced. In the *History of the Greek Nation* Nikolaos Platon concludes, cautiously: "...The scholars who were initially hesitant in admitting that the decipherment had been accomplished eventually sided with Ventris' supporters. Nevertheless,

there are demurrers who do not conceal their reservations.... Some are totally nega-
tive.... So we could say in conclusion that the entire problem is under scrutiny and will
eventually be decided based on whatever new data future research will bring to light."

One of those who had been unreservedly convinced was Spyros Iakovidis, who introduced
the decipherment of Linear B in his very first courses at the University of Athens in the
early 1970s, thus opening to his students a new dimension in Greek archaeological studies.

In all this fascinating story of the decipherment of Linear B, the big winner was John
Chadwick. It was he who completed the research, wrote books that were very successful,
was acclaimed by his fellow scholars, was awarded doctorates by various universities,
and all in all achieved considerable fame. The unluckiest one was Alice Kober; she died,

GEORGE MYLONAS

without even knowing how much she had contributed to this great work. As for Ventris, his name is definitively associated with the decipherment of Linear B—innumerable publications, both scholarly and popular, have celebrated this brilliant amateur and his achievement.

Chance, with its strange convolutions, had Ventris making his famous BBC announcement just a few days after the world was once more dazzled by the opulence and beauty of Mycenaean gold with the dramatic finds in a new grave circle that had been discovered in Mycenae! All Greek newspapers had the news on their front pages—the astonishing chance find of Yiannis Papadimitriou, Ephor of Antiquities for the Argolid and Corinth. There were photographs everywhere; the King and Queen of Greece, Paul and Frederica, went to Mycenae on the twenty-first of June to see the excavation; decorations were conferred; and the Archaeological Society, because of the great importance of the find, appointed a committee of the leading prehistorians at the time, professors Antonios Keramopoulos, Spyridon Marinatos, and George Mylonas, to assist Yiannis Papadimitriou. Mycenae was becoming once more the epicenter of attention, on all counts.

ENTER BOB McCABE WITH HIS CAMERA

It is therefore not strange that in 1954 Bob McCabe had photographed this prehistoric acropolis so minutely, nor that, upon his return to Princeton, he was asked by the department of Graphic Arts of the great library of the university, the Firestone, to offer his photographs for an exhibition on Greece. A few months later, the head of that department, Gillett Griffin, had an idea for another exhibition—this time about the decipherment of Linear B. There too they used many of the same Mycenae photographs you see in the book you are now holding, the only difference being that then the students had the amusing inspiration to write the captions in Linear B!

A few blocks from Princeton University is the Institute for Advanced Study, where scholars are invited to stay for a few months and pursue their research undistracted. Among them, in 1954, was the Greek epigraphist George Stamiris, whom Bob McCabe had already met in Greece. Alan Wace was also a guest in residence at the Institute. Stamiris introduced McCabe to Wace and McCabe invited Wace to the opening of the exhibition. McCabe recalls:

> To everyone's delight he came. I remember clearly his lanky, slightly slouched stance and how he had his hands clasped behind his back as he very carefully examined each photograph and each element of the exhibition. At one point, he

The back of the Lion Gate. The man in the middle is Aristotle, the guard of the site for many years (in his uniform with cap), talking with the workmen restoring the walls.

gestured towards one of the captions in Linear B and said for all to hear, "That's misspelled!" Our hearts sank until we realized that he really enjoyed the idea that we had tried to write in Linear B, even though we had misspelled a word. Sometime after that Professor Wace contacted me and invited me to photograph Mycenae in detail during the summer of 1955 digging season. I was flattered and elated at the prospect and felt very honored. There was an extraordinary bonus as well: Professor and Mrs. Wace invited me to join them for a week visiting archaeological sites in the Peloponnese. To take us around, he hired an Athenian cab whose driver he seemed to know well. The central focus of the trip was to find the Palace of Menelaus, with a second goal to visit Carl Blegen at Pylos and see the bathtub he had just discovered. Some of the stops were quite off the beaten track, like Vapheio. We spent a lot of time hiking in the area south of Sparta where the Palace was thought to be but did not find anything encouraging.

There were some memorable episodes during our motor tour. One day in Nauplion while the Waces were taking a siesta I rented a motorbike so I could visit Asine, a place mentioned in passing by Homer in the *Iliad*. I arrived, took a few photos, and began heading back to Nauplion to meet up with the Waces and continue the journey. A few miles later, the rear fender of the motorbike broke loose, slid under the tire, and sent me completely out of control. I went flying through the air to a very hard landing on the asphalt. I was cut and bleeding from my forehead and elbows but managed to flag down a small truck. The driver helped me in, then loaded the mangled motorbike onto the bed of the truck. When we got back to the hotel, the Waces were waiting in the lobby for me. Mrs. Wace took one horrified look and said, "We've got to get you to the Americans at Lerna for first aid." So we took off for Lerna, on the other side of the gulf. There we met Lloyd Cotsen, who was working for Professor Caskey. Lloyd became a very close friend. I served on his board at Neutrogena and he became the President of the board of the American School of Classical Studies at Athens.

It was a unique experience, travelling with Professor Wace. I was amazed at his knowledge of the terrain and history of the Peloponnese. He had a story for every stone it seemed. Sometimes when we stopped he would talk about the area where we were and some of the local people would gather to listen.

At Pylos there was the famous bathtub, newly discovered. When Professor Blegen heard I was a photographer he made sure that my camera was not allowed to come near the bathtub! Professor Wace explained that he was afraid I might give the image to be published.

It was at Pylos that I took the photo of Piet de Jong drawing a pot. It's one of my favorite images.

When we returned to Mycenae I spent more than a week taking photos of the site. I climbed Zara, not realizing what I had gotten into—no paths, little light coming down at dusk. And I climbed partway up Mount Profitis Ilias, coming upon the shepherd's camp with a baby's cradle.

I remember the bees like it was yesterday—many bees, dozens of bees, buzzing around our breakfast, which took place at dawn inside a Mycenaean tomb (which in Greek is called a *tholos* and in English much more aptly, a beehive tomb). Our breakfast consisted of bread, figs, and honey, which may explain the bees' interest. I will never forget Mrs. Wace, who one morning saw me trying to peel a fig, and making all eyes focus on my awkward attempts, turned to Charles Williams and said "Charles! Show Robert how to peel his fig." Today, after sixty years, I remember this every time I eat a fig.

In the more than thirty centuries of Mycenae's history, the thirty years between 1930 and 1960 can, I believe, be considered a landmark. It took the Mycenaeans two centuries to mature; two centuries of greatness followed, then a century of decline, and a century of collapse; then they disappeared, sunk into oblivion, for more than twenty centuries. Of the Achaean world, its seats of power, its network of influences, its conquests and accomplishments—what was left were only a few names and deeds which were ascribed to Homer's poetic fantasy.

But suddenly, at the end of the nineteenth century AD, Mycenaean civilization escapes from the realm of myth and enters decisively into the realm of prehistory, while just a few decades later, in the momentous thirty-year period between 1930 and 1960, it moves on from prehistory into protohistory, thanks to the decipherment of Linear B.

In 1939, approximately fifteen years before these photographs were taken, and in the same year Vronwy Hankey made her observations, the American writer Henry Miller looked upon these same antiquities. He arrived at a different time of the day than the McCabe brothers and at another time of year: in the morning other colors clothed the Mycenaean acropolis and the fields were, at the time, green only in spring. But he too saw a landscape and ancient remains that stirred him profoundly.

In his book *The Colossus of Maroussi*, he relates how they started off on a Sunday morning from Nauplion, probably on the train that then ran between Nauplion and Mycenae:

It was hardly eight o'clock when we arrived at the little station bearing this leg-endary name. Passing through Argos, the magic of this world suddenly penetrat-ed my bowels…. Things long-forgotten came back with frightening clarity. I was not sure whether I was recalling things I had read as a child, or whether I was tapping the universal memory of the race. The fact that these places still existed, still bore their ancient names, seemed incredible…. From the station to the ruins was a walk of several kilometers. As at Epidaurus, there was a sublime stillness all about…. After you pass the little hostelry run by Agamemnon and his wife which faces a field of Irish green, you become immediately aware that the earth is sown with the bodies and the relics of legendary figures…. The approach to the place of horror is fantastically inviting. There are smooth green mounds, hummocks, hillocks, tumuli everywhere, and beneath them, not very deep either, lie the warriors and heroes, the fabulous innovators who without machinery erected the most formidable fortifications.

The acropolis of Mycenae itself appeared to him as the epitome of contradictions, threatening one moment, seductive the next. He says its walls are Cyclopean, its ornaments delicate objects of unrivalled grace in any period of art: "It is one of the navels of human spirit, the place of attachment to the past and of complete severance too."

Henry Miller wrote many more very poetic thoughts, and concluded: "The historians and the archaeologists have woven a slim and altogether unsatisfying fabric to cover the mystery. They piece together fragmentary items which are linked in the customary manner to suit their necessitous logic. Nobody has yet penetrated the secret of this hoary scene."

GIANT STEPS IN ARCHAEOLOGY

Of course ancient landscapes and monuments have always provided enticing unsolved mysteries for writers to marvel at. But the fact is that at this very time—the beginning of our pivotal thirty-year period—in the real world of archaeology, serious research was in felicitous full swing. Exceptional minds, the kind that appear only rarely, had turned to prehistory with a vengeance. Working in collaboration, or on parallel lines, or independently, agreeing or on opposite sides, supporting each other's work or demolishing

it—philologists, excavators, men of letters, even amateurs, on both sides of the Atlantic, honed each other's minds conjecturing and refuting.

Their common passion was the discovery of truth and their tools were the new techniques of archaeological research which were in turn borrowing from developing new technologies. These extraordinary individuals created a fabric which is not "slim and unsatisfying" at all, and finally penetrated the mystery of that "hoary scene" in a very satisfactory way indeed.

And not only did they penetrate the mystery of Mycenae, but, broadening the focus, we see that in the space of a few decades, they brought to light Minoan Crete and the Aegean with Santorini, along with their relations with Asia Minor and the Middle East and Egypt, that is to say they put within the purview of archaeology many centuries of developments, interactions, and conflicts.

But to go back to Mycenae, Spyros Iakovidis, drawing upon the wisdom of all that work undertaken by his predecessors, could in the early seventies summarize the beginnings of the Achaean civilization, as follows:

> The fire that broke out at the Palace of Knossos, a spring day with a strong north wind, a little after 1400 BC, did not turn to ashes only the huge and labyrinthine building. Along with the building, it crippled and disorganized the administrative and economic hub of the island, thus crowning a process of gradual but steady displacement of the center of power from insular Crete to mainland Greece. This process had started much earlier, and the efforts of the Achaean rulers at Knossos

Sophia Kolizera leads two horses along a road in the upper part of the village. The village of Mycenae (then called Charvati) moved in the early eighteenth century from the area of the current car park to its present site further to the south. When excavation resumed in 1950 after the German occupation and the civil war the village was very poor but thanks to imaginative aid—like the import of brood mares in foal—and the wages paid to the villagers who worked on the excavation, it soon started to flourish. The acropolis of Mycenae's ancient enemy Argos is in the background, right.

had not been able to check it. Already towards the end of the fifteenth century BC, the first Mycenaean commercial stations had appeared alongside the major Minoan ones (on Melos, Rhodes, Kythera) evidently bent on displacing them. The Mycenaean products had already begun to appear in the Eastern markets and were competing successfully with Cretan trade.... The Achaeans, or at least some Achaeans, must have already raided the coast of Asia Minor, an area that never ceased to attract them.... Judging from the excavation finds and to a certain extent from the substratum of memories guessed at in the surviving myths and traditions, what emerges is the picture of a new, robust, and expanding world, which, having assimilated elements of the Minoan civilization it had found useful—and especially the organization of a central government and of trade after the model of Eastern cities—was by now ready to oust or oppose those who taught it. The destruction of the palace at Knossos had definitively relegated Crete to the rear, henceforth following and adapting without undertaking significant initiatives. This opened the way for the expansion of Mycenaean commerce, now free and without meaningful competition. (Iakovidis, *The History of the Greek Nation*, vol. I, p. 260.)

THE STRATEGIC ADVANTAGE OF ARIDNESS

The plain of Argos that was seen by Heinrich Schliemann was much the same as the one Miller and McCabe saw: bare mountains, meager harvests, mud-brick houses, misery, infertility. None of the big rivers of the Peloponnese runs through the narrow plain of Argos, and those mentioned in Antiquity have dwindled to streams that completely dry out in the summer.

Because the land is so parched, the Greeks won one of their greatest battles there during their War of Independence. The month was July and the year 1822. Dramalis, leading some 30,000 Turkish soldiers, was advancing against the Greek revolutionaries who had conquered Tripoli. The Greeks, unable as they were to match his numbers, allowed him virtually unchallenged to pass Corinth. They delayed him at Argos. Then they cut off the roads towards Tripoli, which was his objective. They cornered him in a poor area, where the locals took it upon themselves—by burning crops and polluting wells—to make it even more destitute. His soldiers started going hungry and even worse, going thirsty, both themselves and their horses. There was nothing left for him but to turn back to Corinth—with its storehouses and abundant water supplies. Kolokotronis knew now where he should lay in wait for Dramalis: together with a handful of men they seized the Dervenakia pass, the only way out of the Argolid towards Corinth, and there they fell upon the Turkish army and crushed it.

Today, a modern Kolokotronis could not have done the same, because now the Argolid is a large, well-watered orchard, full of fruits and vegetables and herds of goats and sheep and wealthy farmers living in tall spacious houses with all the modern amenities. The Argolid has no rivers, but it has abundant subterranean waters, which gather from the mountains to the west. When irrigation through drilling was introduced after the war, grain cultivation gradually disappeared from the plain and was replaced by orange and other citrus trees, which are much easier and more profitable to grow. Poverty was left behind and today is forgotten.

MYLONAS MAKES A DIFFERENCE

This change, however, took many years to materialize and in the meantime, in 1953, another man arrived at Mycenae, a man who, like Tsountas and Wace, was more than a great archaeologist. George Mylonas, professor at Washington University in St. Louis, was the one who would very soon take over as the director of the excavations at Mycenae; but he also bound himself closely to the village itself and helped advance its prospects.

Mylonas, like Tsountas, was also born and brought up in a town which, although outside the frontiers of Greece, had a very ancient Hellenic culture and a flourishing Greek population. But there was a difference: Tsountas could, if he wanted, return to his hometown, Stenimachos, while Mylonas had seen his own hometown, Smyrna, go up in flames before he himself was taken prisoner by the Turks in 1922. He was one of the few lucky ones who survived. Wearing a sack, held up at the shoulders by two safety pins, he eventually reached Piraeus. He got work as a bricklayer in the construction of the Gennadius Library, a part of the American School of Classical Studies at Athens, and ended up a world-famous archaeologist, a member of the Academy of Athens, and an eminent excavator of Mycenae.

I think that if he had not been so cruelly uprooted, Mylonas may not have put so much care and effort into that miserable village at the foot of the acropolis of Mycenae. If there had been some other place that he and his wife (also a refugee from Asia Minor) could call their own homeland, they would not have created at Mycenae, on a low hill, a small paradise, nor would they have decided to be buried in this village.

In any case, when the Archaeological Society put him in charge of the excavation of Mycenae, Mylonas had already had a brilliant career. After receiving his doctorate from the University of Athens in 1927, he became a professor at the University of Chicago and later, for many years, at Washington University in Saint Louis. In 1951–52 he taught at the American School of Classical Studies at Athens and in 1954 in the Department of Philosophy at the University of Athens.

Sought after for lectures all over the world, a most methodical scholar, a charismatic speaker, an excellent organizer, and very urbane, he knew how to instill enthusiasm in his students and to keep them as friends of archaeology and of Greece, long after they had graduated from the university. During the German occupation of Greece Mylonas

The village cemetery at the old church of St. George.

did a lot of work for the Greek War Relief Association, collecting money from Greek communities in the States to provide food for the starving Greeks. He put to use all his many talents and extensive connections, and thanks to the donations of his American students and friends, he created the Mycenaean Foundation with the aim of funding the excavators in Mycenae and erecting a building that would house them.

It had become obvious that the excavations at Mycenae were not a matter of one season or even of ten or fifty, or only one generation of archaeologists. The site is vast and extends far beyond the walls, the phases are many, and the information gathered from any one point is invaluable. The archaeologist-excavators would have a permanent presence here, therefore they should have a place for their living quarters, their offices, and a library on the spot.

The Melathron, as Mylonas named it, is a stone building, simple and of pleasing proportions, next to which there is the McCarthy House, or Melathraki (little Melathron), as it is usually called. George Mylonas resided at the Melathron during the excavation period, which lasted the whole summer. Daybreak would find him already at the excavations; at midday work stopped. He would then come back for lunch and rest. In the afternoon he used to come out to the inner atrium and, seated on his chaise longue, entertain his many visitors with stories from his life. All those who had helped him in his career—and they were many—he mentioned often with feeling and humor.

The Melathraki, next door, had as temporary residents any students or researchers who happened to be working that year in Mycenae; and it had one permanent one, Spyros Iakovidis, who was successively assistant, collaborator, co-director, and finally, after Mylonas' death in 1988, director of the excavation until June 2013 and his own death.

Mylonas had a special gift for putting together people, ideas, opportunities, and then making things happen. He envisaged a constructive relationship between the archaeologists and the village. He was not the first. Tsountas had encouraged the farmers to cultivate the olive tree, thus increasing their income. Yiannis Papadimitriou had helped the village acquire basic touristic facilities. Mylonas went even further. He made space at the Melathron for the offices of the community of Mycenae and for a medical clinic that the Mycenaean Foundation equipped generously; he also offered the village use of the central hall of the Melathron for lectures, feast days, and other activities. It so happened that the then-head of the community, George Kolizeras, realizing how much the village could profit from the archaeological site and the archaeologists, became a loyal and lifelong friend of Mylonas and of archaeology. His wife, daughters, and Costas Costouros, his son-in-law, followed his example, although things are now reversed. In the 1960s the archaeologists had something to offer to the poverty-stricken village whereas today the village is no longer a small community but belongs to an extensive municipality. Kolizeras became a very successful businessman; his family now owns one of the largest, best organized, and most attractive restaurants in the area, while the entire village is profiting every year from the thousands of visitors who arrive in groups or on their own to see the acropolis of Mycenae.

MYCENAE AND TOURISM

Tourism in Greece was taking its first steps in the 1950s. Within the same years that Linear B was deciphered and Grave Circle B with its impressive gold finds was discovered, the King and Queen of Greece had organized a highly publicized cruise for royalty in the Aegean on the ship "Agamemnon," offered by the Nomikos family. Also in these years Karamanlis started building the "Xenia" hotels; an excellent school for the training of archaeological guides was established; the first tourist agencies were created; and cruises in the islands and bus tours were now organized professionally.

From the start Mycenae was among the most sought-after destinations. The distance of the site from Athens, which was the hub of touristic activity, was such that groups could only reach it late in the morning. And of course, after visiting the acropolis, they would stay for lunch. With the flexibility peculiar to the Greeks, the modern villagers turned quickly from farmers to restauranteurs, and the once unique Belle Helene suddenly faced stiff competition. Every second family in the village opened a restaurant and strived to make deals with tourist agencies to acquire a permanent flow of customers, and constantly improved their facilities in an attempt to enlarge their share of the market, which anyway was gradually growing.

If Henry Miller saw Mycenae today, he would not recognize either the plain or the village. And if his eyes were trained, he would be surprised by the changes on the acropolis itself, because, although the stone walls have not moved from their place, whole areas have now been uncovered—buildings, staircases, roads—that until a few years ago were invisible, buried under tons of earth.

IAKOVIDIS RECAPITULATES

In 1987 the Archaeological Society celebrated 150 years of existence. It had been 146 years since the Society had sent Kyriakos Pittakis to conduct a preliminary investigation at Mycenae. Commemorating the occasion, Spyros Iakovidis summarized the work that had been done during those years: identification and arrangement of buildings; stratigraphic confirmation of successive phases; discovery of the Processional Way; uncovering of the remains of the palatial building and its annexes, as well as of the Cult Center, chamber tombs, and shaft graves (both inside and outside the walls); and studies of the fortifications of houses outside the acropolis, of five kilometers of Mycenaean road to the east, and many other remains of the Mycenaean, Geometric, Archaic, Hellenistic, and Roman periods. All these, excavated and recorded according to what were by then highly developed excavation techniques, as well as the demands of archaeological science, allowed him to relate Mycenae's history as follows:

The first occupation of the hill of Mycenae begins in Neolithic times. From this phase and continuing on to the next one, the Early Helladic period, we only have scattered pottery finds. After the settlement of the first Greek peoples in 2000 BC, the habitation of the site becomes denser, as attested by the ubiquitous sherds, the architectural remains, and the tombs. The two Grave Circles indicate that the site was already at that time the seat of wealthy and powerful rulers. Of their palace little survived, but their tombs, as well as the tombs of their subjects around the hill, testify to the fact that the population increased steadily, and that both their wealth and quality of life were steadily rising. Mycenae had now embarked on the road to political and economic expansion, which would make it one of the main hegemonies of the Late Bronze Age in Greece, and probably the most powerful. Finally, by the middle of the fourteenth century BC, the fortification wall was built, turning the hill into a fortified acropolis.

A hundred years later the acropolis was extended towards the south and the west and was provided with two fortified gates, one of which was decorated with the Lion relief. Part of the space that was added was dedicated to worship. At the same time, the palatial complex doubled in size, and some buildings, which possibly may have been directly dependent on the palace, were erected outside the walls. A dense network of carriage roads, overseen and protected by closely spaced guard houses, connected the acropolis and the flourishing surrounding area with mainland Greece and the closest ports. Mycenae had become the governing seat of a complex economic and administrative organism, which handled much greater and more varied types of wealth than the region could produce and which was based mainly on transactions with neighboring areas, especially Crete, Egypt, and the commercial centers of the Syro-Palestinian coast.

...A little after the middle of the thirteenth century BC, the acropolis and the surrounding area were struck by a calamity not unknown in the Argolid, a devastating earthquake, that left nothing standing and also caused some local fires.... After the earthquake, efforts started right away to rebuild and repair both inside and, to a certain extent, outside the acropolis. A few years later, at the end of LH IIIB period (circa 1200 BC) isolated but not necessarily simultaneous fires broke out at the Cult Center, at Tsountas' House, at part of the Southwest House, at Panagitsa House II .... and perhaps at the palace. The ruined buildings were cleared once more from the remains of the fire and were repaired.... The twelfth and most of the eleventh century BC was for Mycenae a period of economic withering and political decline, but not one of misery and danger.... The last phase of the Bronze Age at Mycenae passed without general or even extensive destruction and there are no indications of a second earthquake, such as there was at Tiryns.

The archaeological data for the twelfth and the eleventh centuries BC do not substantiate invasions or changes of population on any scale, nor internal turmoil. Mycenae did not come to a violent end and the area never stopped being inhabited. The final abandonment of the acropolis cannot be ascribed to the torch of victorious raiders. It came about as a result of the gradual decline and ultimate break-up of the central government due to the weakening of the palatial economy and administration. This resulted from the troubles of 1200 BC in the Eastern Mediterranean, when the destruction of the commercial harbors cut off the contacts of the palaces in Mycenaean Greece from their main trading partners.

These conclusions were the result of 146 years of intensive archaeological research. Light had been shed on both the beginning and the fall of the Mycenaean world, proving wrong the earlier theories. Work at Mycenae had not finished, nor did any of the excavators see its end as imminent. Nevertheless, it was considered time for a final publication.

PUBLISHING AN EXCAVATION

The word "publication" is deceptive. We say "I publish some news," "I publish an article," and we mean I publicize, I make available for general reading something I have written as I thought best. "I publish an excavation," though, means that I provide the reader in minute detail all the data relative to an excavation, the way it was conducted and the finds upon which my conclusions are based: in this way, every scholar who will read it can have at his disposal all the facts, in order to judge both the methods the excavator employed and the validity of his conclusions.

Publication is a work of precision. It is time-consuming and can only be undertaken when the excavator, after a series of digging seasons, has judged that he has definitely extracted from the earth every single bit of evidence that might illuminate the history of the site.

In order to publish an excavation, the archaeologist will go back to the diaries—his own, those of his predecessors, and/or those of his collaborators—where he will find the detailed and systematic record of the day-to-day actions of all the members of the excavation team. He will draw all the necessary architectural plans and he will photograph all the finds and all related sites; he will make and write down his observations, comparisons, evaluations on the stratigraphy, the texture of the soil, and his comments and conjectures about the possible significance of individual objects or building materials, depending on where they were found and their condition. Finally, based on all this, he will present his conclusions.

Great studies had already been written about Mycenae, by Tsountas (*The Mycenaean Age: A study of the monuments and culture of pre-Homeric Greece*, 1897), Wace (*Excavations at Mycenae*, 1923; *Chamber Tombs at Mycenae*, 1932), and Mylonas (*Mycenae and the Mycenaean Age*, Princeton, NJ, 1966; *Mycenae: Rich in Gold*, Athens 1983; *Mycenae: A Guide to its ruins and its history*, with many photographs and maps); there were also various articles on specific subjects, as well as the Annual Reports submitted by the excavators to the Archaeological Society and published in *Archaeologike Ephemeris* and in the *Praktika*, issued by the Society. Nevertheless, both Mylonas and Iakovidis agreed that the final publication of their finds, as described above, was still pending, and they were ready to begin. But here they faced a serious obstacle: the lack of a secure building to spread out the finds and study them.

Every excavation yields finds. Whether they possess great artistic value or are plain sherds from clay vases, they are all evidence, so they must be cleaned, conserved, drawn, recorded, and safely stored. "An excavation is not like an experiment," Iakovidis used to teach his students, "you cannot repeat it as many times as you wish. Excavation means destruction."

All the objects that the excavator has removed from a specific layer of soil in order to go deeper cannot be placed back in their original position. But all must be preserved, catalogued meticulously and in an orderly way, and stored in accessible places so that they may be examined again whenever needed, and particularly during the preparation of the final publication.

But in Mycenae, because there was no appropriate building, the most spectacular finds were sent to the National Archaeological Museum in Athens, or to the Museum in Nauplion, while the rest were packed up in sacks and were haphazardly placed in small storerooms built for other purposes. There followed impromptu rearrangements: boxes got mixed up, floods and other accidents happened, not to mention the raids of rats who ate the critical descriptive labels tied to the packages.

In spite of the adverse conditions, some important publications had appeared: "The Acropolis of Mycenae" by George Mylonas, in the *Archaiologike Ephemeris* of 1958, "The Acropolis of Mycenae, Part Two: the peribolos walls, the gates, and the ascents," by Mylonas in the 1962 issue of the same journal, as well as the monograph by Artemis Onassoglou "The House of the Tomb of the Tripods at Mycenae" in 1995. But the bulk of the excavation work, conducted over more than 60 years, had yet to be published.

The draftsman and architect Piet de Jong working in the Pylos excavation storeroom in the village of Chora where the excavation team lived. De Jong first met Alan Wace in 1919 and worked with him at Mycenae through 1923.

Antiquities in Greece belong to the State, which has the privilege and the responsibility to exhibit them and keep them safe. If then the State built a Museum at Mycenae, the correct and fair thing to do for such an important archaeological site, the lower floors would automatically house the necessary storerooms and laboratories, and the study period for the final publication could finally begin.

George Mylonas did not have much difficulty convincing the Ministry of Culture about this. The various procedures began; a site was chosen for the Museum on the sloping north side descending to the Kokoretsa stream bed, in the hope that not many important ancient buildings would be encountered there. The clearing of the site and rescue excavations began. And at some point, in the fullness of bureaucratic time after a number of years had gone by, the architects appeared to show their designs to the excavators. The latter had no issues with the proposed exhibition halls, but they were horrified when they saw that the storerooms and laboratories the architects had planned were small rooms, completely unsuitable for their intended use. They complained and once more they explained their needs. Those in charge replied that such extravagance was out of the question! Thus began a building, which would not serve the purpose for which it was originally intended!

THE BENEVOLENT GHOST OF TSOUNTAS

But it seems that Tsountas' spirit still fluttered protectively over Mycenae: the bulldozers arrived at the chosen plot, and started digging for the foundations, reaching for hard ground. The soil they came upon was soft; they went deeper, but again they found soft soil; they went even deeper, again soft soil.... They had come across Tsountas' fill—the tons of soil he had thrown over the acropolis walls towards the great slope to the north, when in one of his many investigations he was disposing of centuries' worth of deposits.

So the Museum had to be adapted to a plot that turned out to be on a steep slope, descending towards the Kokoretsa stream. Thus it got two additional floors, exactly

SPYROS IAKOVIDIS

what was needed for spacious and easily accessible storerooms and laboratories, all comfortable and well-lit.

George Mylonas did not have a chance to work in the Museum that he had fought so many years for. It was still just a skeleton when, in 1988, he died, at a ripe old age, but active 'til the end.

SPYROS IAKOVIDIS TAKES OVER

Spyros Iakovidis, who carried on now on his own, was born in Athens in 1923. He completed his studies at the University of Athens, experiencing all the bloodshed and wasted years that the war and the subsequent internal turmoil cost his generation. Alongside archaeology, he had attended classes at the Polytechnic to learn to do his own plotting, and draw plans to the highest standards of accuracy. A student and admirer of Spyridon Marinatos, he obtained his PhD with a study of the "Mycenaean Acropolis of Athens." His first excavation was a Mycenaean cemetery at Perati, in Attica. It was a model of a prompt and thorough publication, fulfilling the modern conception of what an excavator owes to his successors in completeness and precision. For a few years he accompanied Marinatos in his excavations at Messenia and Santorini, and George Mylonas in his own excavations first at Eleusis and then at Mycenae. From 1953 onwards, he worked alongside Mylonas at Mycenae, first as his assistant, then as his collaborator, later as co-director, and finally as director.

The excavation season at Mycenae, both in Mylonas' and Iakovidis' time, started at the beginning of July and did not end until September, only after all the objects discovered that year had been photographed. Year after year they went on at that same pace, while the completion of the museum was awaited with increasing impatience but without results.

THE ARCHAEOLOGICAL ATLAS OF MYCENAE

In the meantime another major project was initiated. In the beginning of the 1990s, Dr. Lisa Wace French, daughter of Alan Wace and a distinguished archaeologist herself, who was then serving as the Director of the British School at Athens, proposed to the Archaeological Society to join forces for the creation of a comprehensive archaeological atlas of Mycenae. The proposal was accepted and the general direction of the project was entrusted to Spyros Iakovidis.

At the south end of the Panagia ridge Charles Williams (excavation architect 1955) discusses the excavation with the trench master of that area, Reynald Higgins (of the British Museum, later Chairman of the Managing Committee of the British School). The basic "dumpy level" set up for use in surveying the area is very different from the "total station" that would be used today. But the results would be much the same.

"The Mycenae Atlas," says Dr. French, "was a joint project undertaken in the 1990s by Professor Iakovidis and myself in which we recorded onto large-scale maps everything that could be gleaned about the site of Mycenae from publications and notebooks as well as from the actual surface of the site and its surrounding territory. With the assistance of the Archaeological Service and an active support team of students and colleagues of each of us from Pennsylvania, Athens, and Manchester, we surveyed widely and noted all we saw using the latest technology. Over the years I had come to realize that much information that formed an essential foundation to future work was largely inaccessible, often indeed held in the memory of scholars who had worked at the site. My colleague, the redoubtable scholar Barbara Craig (Principal of Somerville College, Oxford), and I had planned and actually started a comprehensive index to publications but the chance to combine this with work at the site itself resulted most gratifyingly in what has become an indispensable tool. Moreover in my own case, it has allowed me to contribute something distinctive of my own to the intimidating legacy of the many archaeologists, including my polymath father Alan Wace, who have excavated at Mycenae over the years. That Mycenae was his favorite site shows clearly in the book he published in 1949, *Mycenae, an Archaeological History and Guide*. This and the collection of short stories set in pre-WWI Greece, entitled *Greece Untrodden*, are perhaps the best he ever wrote and encapsulate the love of Greece felt by British scholars of his time."

The *Archaeological Atlas of Mycenae* consists of a first part, with twelve large maps, drawn to a scale of 1:5000, and many other smaller maps of the surrounding area, where ancient remains have been located. The second part includes the mapping of the acropolis of Mycenae on one sheet drawn to a scale of 1:1000, and other smaller ones, to a scale of 1:400. The maps are accompanied by texts written by Spyros Iakovidis, Lisa French, and the scholars they collaborated with.

The work is monumental. For something similar, one has to go back to 1895, when the Germans drew up and printed the geographical surveys of Attica, "Karten von Attica." On the Internet site of the Society one can read that, "It is the Archaeological Society's first attempt at archaeological mapping." One could also add: It is an important accomplishment, a model of scholarly scrupulousness, and an example of harmonious cooperation amongst many individuals under the auspices of the Society.

PUBLICATIONS

The Museum opened, at last, in the year 2000! Spyros Iakovidis settled into his office there and the preparation of the final publications began. Iakovidis published in a way which his student and collaborator Christos Boulotis, describes as follows:

The various publications of Professor Iakovidis, especially the volumes pertaining to excavations (Perati, Glas, Mycenae), reflect directly, I think, the man himself: a structured personality with a strict scholarly mind and unequalled consistency. The punctilious publication of an excavation was for him more than a duty and a requisite; it was, by conviction, his only way of existing inside the archaeological universe of his time. A firm believer in the principle that each archaeological "event" is, by definition, an act of destruction, in the sense that it is a unique act which cannot be replicated at will, the way an experiment can, he kept as a privileged but also responsible "eyewitness" exemplary diaries, aiming at a reconstruction on paper of the overall picture of the excavation. Unstintingly he noted down everything, thousands of measurements, calculations, detailed descriptions, observations, correlations *in situ*. He never wavered from his belief that even the smallest detail acquired a voice within the context of the excavation that it could speak and substantiate. No single thing that the earth has kept for us and the archaeological pick has brought back to the light, should fall back into oblivion. His skill in architectural design enabled him to plot maps in his own hand, thus adding a dimension to his on-the-spot observations, and this helped him to better understand each find. Knowing well how much equivocation, controversy, and interpretational misunderstanding the excavational practices of the end of the nineteenth and beginning of the twentieth centuries had bequeathed to us, he adopted the exact opposite methodology, without seeking to impress and without doubtful theorizing. The beginning, for him, was the excavation, the find, on which he firmly based his interpretations and the few global syntheses he at times attempted.

The four volumes published about Mycenae, starting from the year 2006, follow a uniform structure: one part is the description of the buildings and the finds, a second part is the systematic section, that is the study by sections: the foundations, the walls, the floors, etc. In the end there is an extensive summary in English.

The first volume, "The Northwest Quarter," he undertook on his own. The second volume, "The Workshop at Mycenae," dealing with the area where the museum had been built, haphazardly and hurriedly excavated in 1979, he assigned to Dr. Despina Danielidou, who had been an assistant of George Mylonas, and would later become his own invaluable one. Her work, as he writes in the introduction to the volume, "was a feat that surpassed his expectations." The third volume, "The Southwest Quarter," was a collective work with Kim Shelton-Dimopoulou, his former student and assistant, and now professor at the University of California, Berkeley, and the archaeologists participating in the project, each specializing in a different field: Despina Danielidou, Christophilis Maggidis, Tina Bolotis, Vasso Pliatsika, and Iphigenia Tournavitou. The publication of one more volume, dealing with buildings Delta and Gamma, in the East Wing of the palatial complex, was entrusted to Nagia Sgouritsa, his old student and former assistant at the University of Athens, now a professor herself.

Iakovidis died unexpectedly in June 2013, before he had the chance to give the go-ahead for the printing of the fourth volume of the Mycenae series, entitled "The House at Plakes," which he had already written and submitted to the Archaeological Society. Vasileios Petrakos, a member of the Academy of Athens and General Secretary of the Society, who had for decades worked closely with Iakovidis and had become a close friend, assigned the final editing to Electra Andreadi, who knew him well and had edited many of his books. The index was created by the archaeologist Orestis Goulakos, and Christos Boulotis assumed responsibility for the identification of the fragments of wall-paintings illustrated in the book. So the volume came out without delay and as the author had wished.

These volumes of course are not the last word on Mycenae. But they do illustrate exceptionally well how archaeology has evolved in the years since Schliemann into a scientific, multidisciplinary field. With new technologies we can expect the trend to continue, enhancing and augmenting the information that will be gleaned through future excavations.

p. 88
Alan Wace looking out from the Lion Gate toward the roads leading north past some of the richest cemeteries of Mycenae.

If you happen to visit Mycenae today, with this book in hand, you will be able to see the place, the people, and the very progress of archaeology—simultaneously at three different moments in time. You will be delighted by this impressive site with its glorious and bloodthirsty ancient myths, the astonishing changes in nature and in the life of its inhabitants, and also the epic efforts of the human mind to draw out of the darkness more than ten centuries of two highly complex civilizations.

Sixty years have gone by since that summer in 1954, when Bob McCabe took the first of the photos displayed in this book. Before that sixty years had passed since, at the end of the nineteenth century AD, research on Mycenaean civilization began. Thus the year 1954 marks the halfway point along a course of more than 100 years. It also marks its turning point.

In 1954 the conditions for the rapid and multilateral change that was coming had already been created: in a few years the Argive plain, dry for centuries, would become green once more. In a few years, poverty would disappear. The modern Mycenaeans, from being exclusively farmers, would also become restaurant owners, and the entire area would acquire an air of affluence. And also, within the space of a few years, with the decipherment of Linear B, Mycenaean civilization would pass at one go from prehistory to protohistory; its ascent and its decline would be examined with the modern tools of archaeological science and the recording and analyses of excavations would take a new turn towards clarity and accuracy.

It is this crucial moment in time that Bob McCabe has captured with his lens. And since the passage of time also implies change and destruction, these photographs, apart from their undeniable aesthetic value, hold the additional fascination of evidence: they fix on paper a reality that, unaltered for centuries, would soon vanish.

PLANS OF THE ACROPOLIS OF MYCENAE
AND SOME FINDS FROM THE EXCAVATIONS

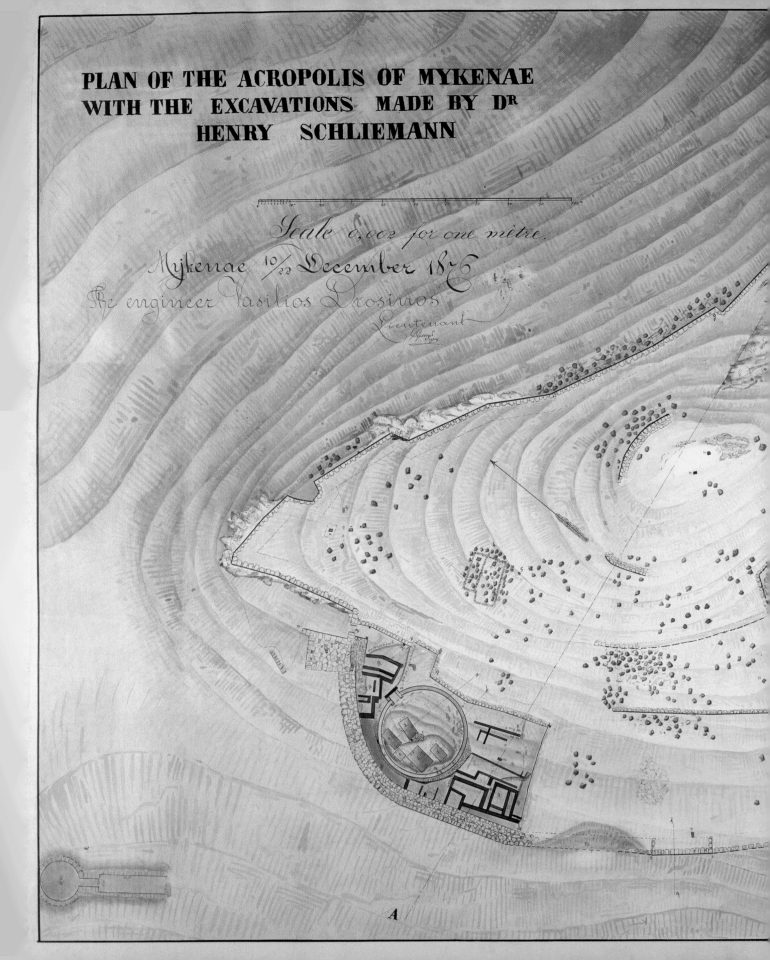

PLAN OF THE ACROPOLIS OF MYKENAE WITH THE EXCAVATIONS MADE BY DR HENRY SCHLIEMANN

Scale 0,002 for one mètre.

Mykenae 10/22 December 1876

The engineer Vasilios Drosinos

Lieutenant

A

Plan II

I. PLATE

B

This evocative plan of the Acropolis of Mycenae was drawn in 1876 by Vasileios Drosinos, a civil engineer from Nauplion. Drosinos reported to the site on November 5, 1876 to start work, having been hired by Schliemann a few days earlier. The plan brings to life the earliest days of archaeological work at Mycenae, with just Grave Circle A and the immediately surrounding area excavated. This manuscript was the basis for the engraved plan that appears in Schliemann's "Mycenae" published by John Murray in 1878. Today the manuscript is in the collection of the National Library of Scotland. We are grateful to the Trustees of the Library for permission to reproduce it.

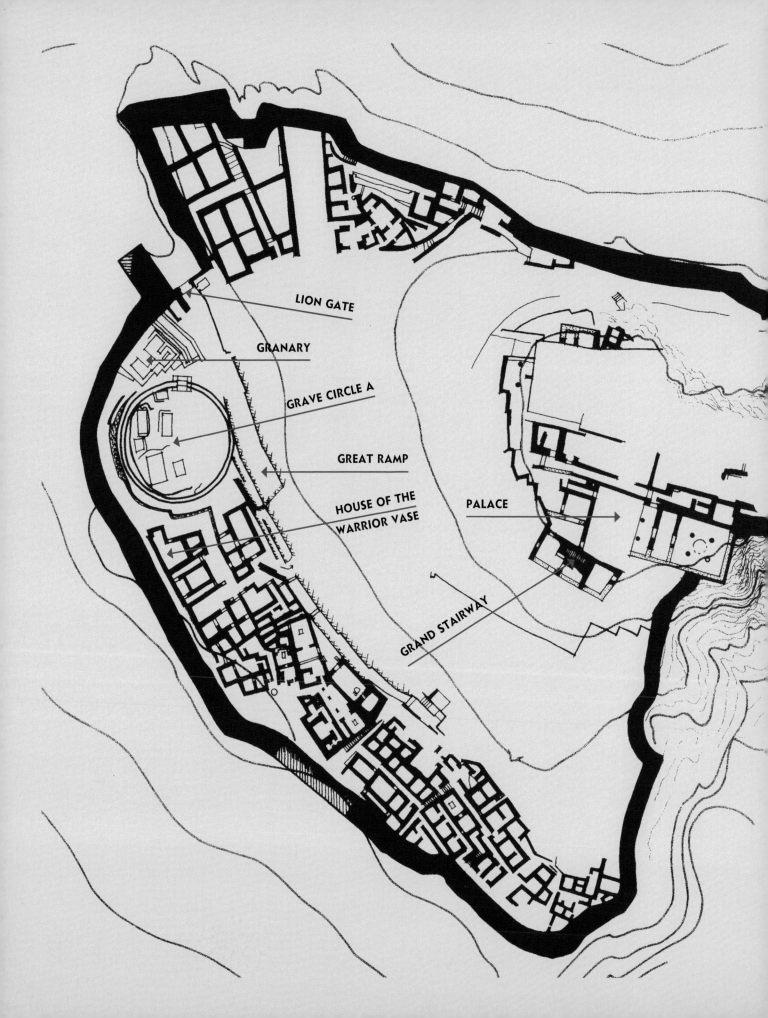

LION GATE

GRANARY

GRAVE CIRCLE A

GREAT RAMP

HOUSE OF THE
WARRIOR VASE

PALACE

GRAND STAIRWAY

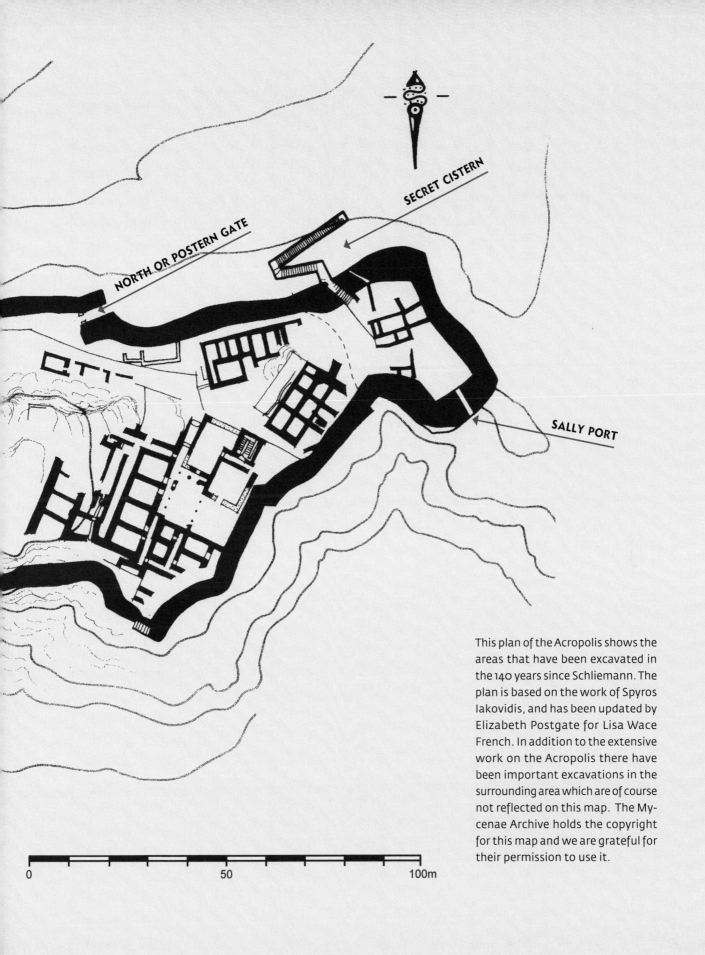

NORTH OR POSTERN GATE

SECRET CISTERN

SALLY PORT

0   50   100m

This plan of the Acropolis shows the areas that have been excavated in the 140 years since Schliemann. The plan is based on the work of Spyros Iakovidis, and has been updated by Elizabeth Postgate for Lisa Wace French. In addition to the extensive work on the Acropolis there have been important excavations in the surrounding area which are of course not reflected on this map. The Mycenae Archive holds the copyright for this map and we are grateful for their permission to use it.

The Mask of Agamemnon. Found in Grave Circle A and named by Schliemann. The name has stuck although the mask is dated some 400 years before currently accepted dates for Agamemnon. National Archaeological Museum, Athens. Giannis Patrikianos photo.

Gold death mask. Found in Grave Circle A. National Archaeological Museum, Athens. Giannis Patrikianos photo.

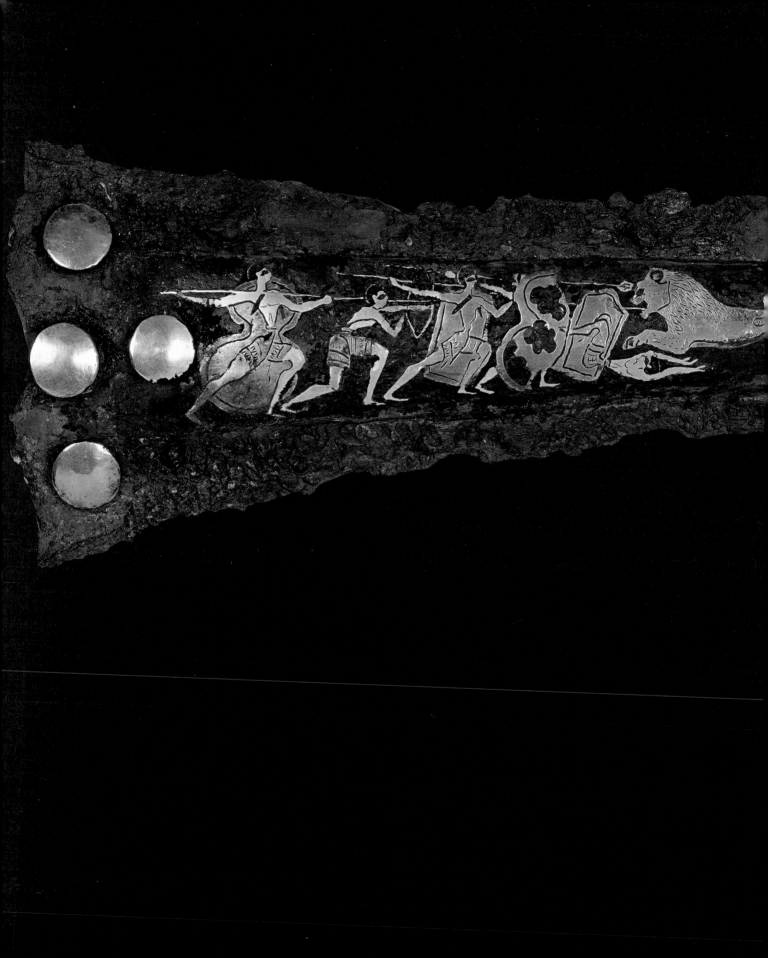

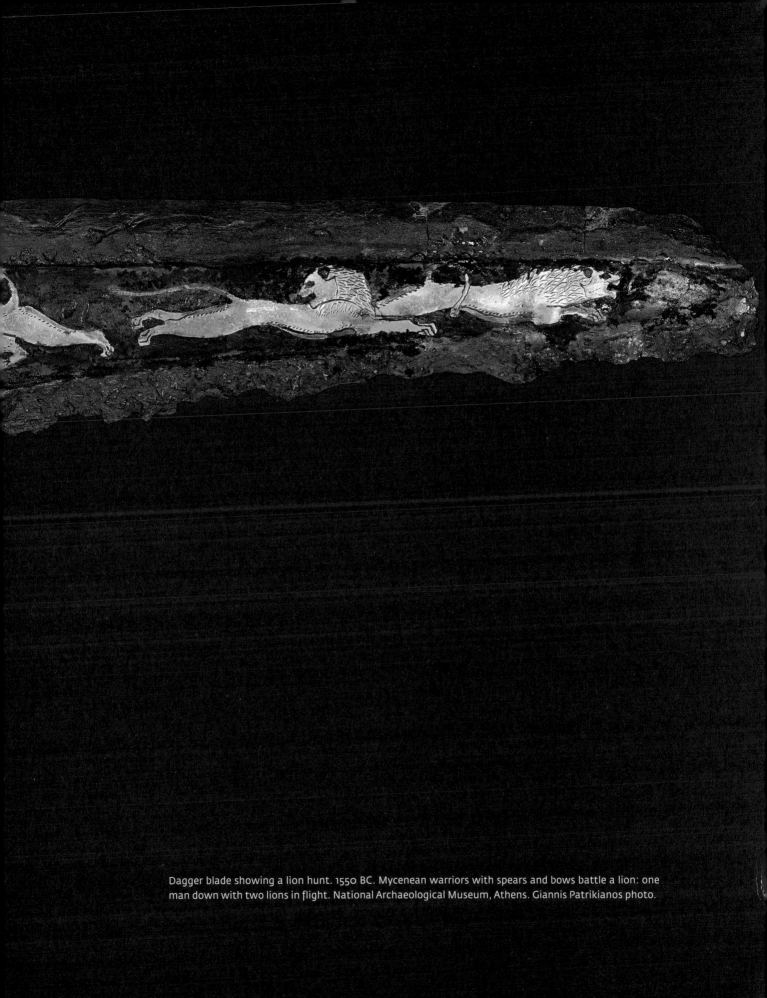

Dagger blade showing a lion hunt. 1550 BC. Mycenean warriors with spears and bows battle a lion: one man down with two lions in flight. National Archaeological Museum, Athens. Giannis Patrikianos photo.

Warrior Vase. Ca. 1150 BC. This vase was produced very late in Mycenae's Bronze Age life. The armor depicted is generally considered a post-Trojan War type. National Archaeological Museum, Athens. Giannis Patrikianos photo.

Ivory statuette of two women with a child. Found in the Palace. 2 ¾" high. National Archaeological Museum, Athens. Kostas Xenikakis photo.

Rock crystal *kymbe*. Found in Grave Circle B. This duck-shaped bowl for cosmetics was carved from a single piece of rock crystal. It is generally regarded as of Minoan origin. National Archaeological Museum, Athens. Kostas Xenikakis photo.

Gold long-stem cup with dog's head handles. Found in Grave Circle A. National Archaeological Museum, Athens.

Gold cup with single handle and scalloped edges. Found in Midea, a few miles from Mycenae. National Archaeological Museum, Athens. National Archaeological Museum Archives photo.

Gold cup with spiral pattern. Found in Grave Circle A. National Archaeological Museum, Athens. Giannis Patrikianos photo.

Small gold amphora with a lid. Found in Grave Circle A. National Archaeological Museum, Athens. RM photo.

Octopus cup. Found in Midea. 1400 BC. The octopus was a common theme in Minoan and Mycenean vase painting. National Archaeological Museum, Athens. RM photo.

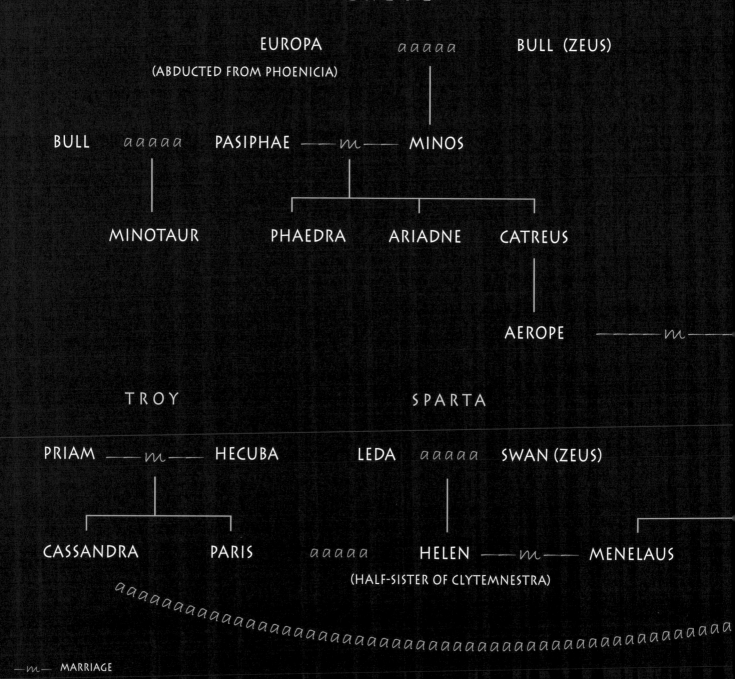

CRETE

EUROPA *aaaaa* BULL (ZEUS)
(ABDUCTED FROM PHOENICIA)

BULL *aaaaa* PASIPHAE ——m—— MINOS

MINOTAUR   PHAEDRA   ARIADNE   CATREUS

AEROPE ——————————m——

TROY   SPARTA

PRIAM ——m—— HECUBA   LEDA *aaaaa* SWAN (ZEUS)

CASSANDRA   PARIS   *aaaaa*   HELEN ——m—— MENELAUS
                            (HALF-SISTER OF CLYTEMNESTRA)

——m— MARRIAGE

aaaaa AFFAIR

| DESCENT

TREE

MYCENAE

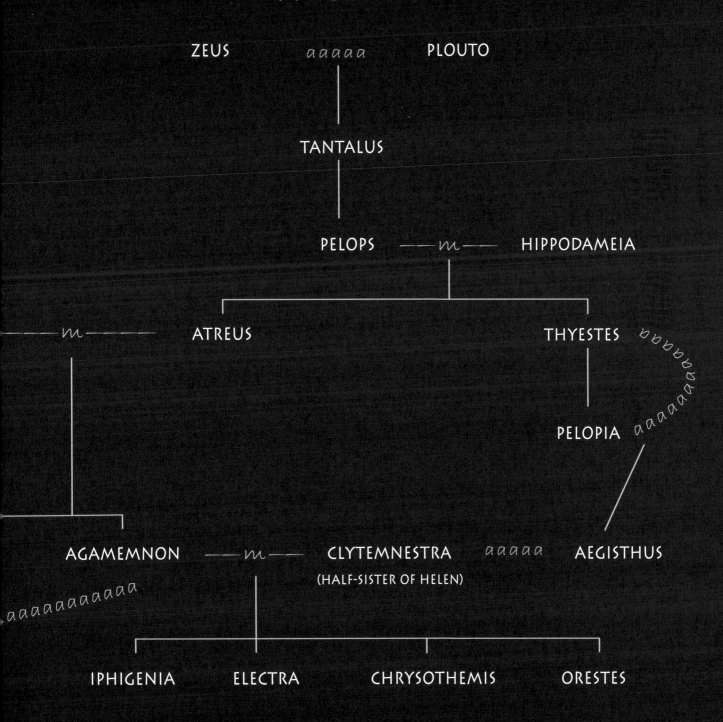

ZEUS ————— aaaaa ————— PLOUTO

TANTALUS

PELOPS ——— m ——— HIPPODAMEIA

——— m ——— ATREUS   THYESTES aaaaaaaaaa

PELOPIA aaaaaaaaaa

AGAMEMNON ——— m ——— CLYTEMNESTRA aaaaa AEGISTHUS
(HALF-SISTER OF HELEN)

aaaaaaaaaaa

IPHIGENIA   ELECTRA   CHRYSOTHEMIS   ORESTES

JOHN GUARE

WAR BRIDE

THE TRAGIC STORY
OF AGAMEMNON KING OF MYCENAE
AND CASSANDRA PRINCESS OF TROY
ON THE OCCASION OF THEIR
SEA JOURNEY FROM TROY

On the deck of a ship.
AGAMEMNON, 50. CASSANDRA, 20. SHE laughs.

A: What in god's name do you find to laugh about? This ship is still scarred from war. A storm could come out of the sea at any moment and swivel us into the underworld.

C: I'm laughing at a blank.

A: A blank? What are you saying?

C: I'm laughing at the wonder of seeing nothing. Apollo cursed me with the future. I could see the future and no one would believe me. But now, for the first time in years, I see nothing. The curse is lifted. I'm free! Don't you think that's funny?

A: I never took you seriously.

C: Did Apollo change his mind? Or does his power not travel beyond Troy?

A: You're a slave. I'll tell you when you can speak.

C: A slave? Is that what I finally am? My position was very ambiguous back there.

A: It's very clear. You're my slave.

C: And I thought when we left I was your war bride.

A: Pillow talk. You're a spoil. A spoil of war. A souvenir. A snow globe. A demi-tasse cup with the words 'I heart Troy' painted across it.

C: And here I thought you were bringing home your war bride. No wonder I laugh. I can't trust men. I can't trust Apollo. I thought at least he'd have the courage of his curses. His curse was the one dependable thing in my life.

A: You can't see the future?

C: I'm just like you.

A: But that's what I liked about you.

C: I could see the future?

A: I found the rumor of it very attractive.

C: But the curse is no one would believe me.

A: It made you vulnerable. A charming curse.

C: And now it's gone.

Painted plaster head of a woman. 1300 BC. National Archaeological Museum, Athens. Giannis Patrikianos photo.

A: Since when?

C: I knew it when we got on this ship.

A: Why didn't you say anything?

C: I was afraid you only loved me for my curse.

A: Knowing the future is a powerful tool. Everyone's afraid of you. If it's true, it'll be our little secret.

C: So now that I'm like everybody else, do you want to throw me overboard?

A: Why? You fit into the symmetry of victory. Ten years ago your brother kidnapped my brother's wife. Ten years later I bring home the kidnapper's sister. Victory loves symmetry.

C: Home? I don't have a home.

A: Your new home. Wait! The air just changed. We're close to home. I own this air. Learn this air. Suck it in. This is your air. The air. The air. Breathe deep.

C: All my nose picks up is the memory of smoke. Burning flesh. Defeat. I'm so used to the smoke in my past I no longer bother to cough. My lungs have come to terms with the smell of burning flesh and dead brothers. My father's dead body. Did you kill him?

A: No. Achilles' son, Pyrrhus.

C: See, not only can I no longer see the future, I can't even remember who killed my dad. I believe I had fifty brothers. Are they all dead?

A: I assume so.

Boar tusk helmet found at Mycenae. Ca. 1400 BC. National Archaeological Museum, Athens. Kostas Xenikakis photo.

"Meriones gave Odysseus a bow, a quiver, and a sword, and put a cleverly made leather helmet on his head. On the inside there was a strong lining on interwoven straps, onto which a felt cap had been sewn. The outside was cleverly adorned all around with rows of white tusks from a shiny-toothed boar, the tusks running in alternate directions in each row."

Μηριόνης δ᾿ Ὀδυσῆϊ δίδου βιὸν ἠδὲ φαρέτρην / καὶ ξίφος, ἀμφὶ δέ οἱ κυνέην κεφαλῆφιν ἔθηκε / ῥινοῦ ποιητήν· πολέσιν δ᾿ ἔντοσθεν ἱμᾶσιν / ἐντέτατο στερεῶς· ἔκτοσθε δὲ λευκοὶ ὀδόντες / ἀργιόδοντος ὑὸς θαμέες ἔχον ἔνθα καὶ ἔνθα / εὖ καὶ ἐπισταμένως· μέσσῃ δ᾿ ἐνὶ πῖλος ἀρήρει.

— Homer, Iliad 10.260–5

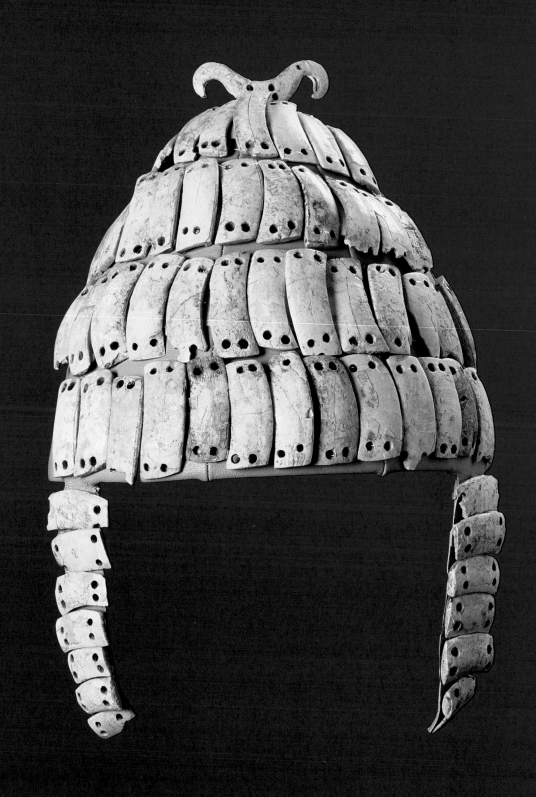

C: Fifty brothers and no one to rescue me. When I had my curse, I would've known whether or not I'd be rescued.

A: Why did you rebuff Apollo? I'd think getting him in your bed would have been a feather in your cap.

C: I don't like feathers and I never wear a cap. Sure I promised to go to bed with him, but I never intended to. And when he realized it, he punished me by not letting anyone believe my forecasts. At least his father Zeus had a creative flair and prided himself on becoming the shape of whatever the woman he was pursuing dreamed. Europa dreamed of a bull. Zeus became a bull. Danae was money mad. Zeus transformed into a shower of gold with a penis. Leda dreamed violent dreams of swans. Zeus became a swan and fathered your sister-in-law whom my brother kidnapped. Like father like son? Hardly. His little boy Apollo was so full of himself he thought he could get anyone in bed with a snap of his fingers.

A: Is it true that after Apollo left you, you went to the docks and slept in broad daylight with a sailor on leave?

C: Yes.

A: Why?

C: He was from a place I'd never been. I wanted to know what Egypt tasted like.

A: No wonder Apollo cursed you.

C: It wasn't even a particularly good curse. 'Oh scary she can see the future.'

A: So what could Apollo have turned into to unclasp your legs since you seem to admire his daddy Zeus' creativity? Might be good for me to know.

C: My dream?

A: Your shower of gold. Your swan.

C: Tell you?

A: Zeus is my great-great-grandfather.

C: Then I'm certainly not going to tell one of his relatives.

A: I don't know why but I'm happy Apollo lifted his curse. It was too alarming being in constant touch with the future.

C: Maybe he lifted it because there is no more future. The sea. The sky. No horizon. High noon. No shadow. No horizon. This is it. We skim over the sea. Suspended. So calm. Are we moving?

A: We speed over the sea and the wind has changed. I'm smiling. Do you know how long it's been since I have smiled?

C: Hold on to that smile. Remember that smile.

A: Did the future just tell you something?

C: Don't be frightened. I'm being realistic. Tell me where I'm going? See? In the old days I'd know.

A: Mycenae.

C: Is it green? Is it brown? Is it rocky? Is it dry? Is it on the sea?

A: All of the above.

C: Who are your people?

A: Why do you want to know?

C: Since I no longer know the future, I want to know everyone's past. You're the king?

A: I was when I left.

C: Will you still sleep with me?

A: You'd be disappointed if I didn't.

C: Not necessarily. You make love as if you're the best thing that will happen to me today.

A: I can't be selfish. I've given you pain. Now the war is over. I'll give you joy.

C: Your wife.

A: What about my wife?

C: Will she welcome me as a royal concubine?

A: She's very understanding. At least she was. You'll like your new family. You're definitely moving up.

C: I was a princess of the house of Priam.

A: The house of Priam? Red necks. As I understand it, your father's high moment was doing battle with some Amazons. But my people! It's quite a family you're joining.

C: I heard the rowers talking about the illustrious house of Atreus.

A: I prefer to call us the house of Tantalus. My great-grandfather Tantalus was the son of Zeus. So you are coming up in the world.

C: It didn't do anything for Apollo. What is it like to be stuck with Zeus for a dad?

A: Apparently Zeus was quite available. He was proud of a son whose mother was a sea nymph. All the gods liked Tantalus. They'd say playfully, "We could eat you up." When Tantalus came of age with the birth of his son, Pelops, Zeus said, "Tantalus, let's celebrate the new generation with a feast fit for the gods." Tantalus decided the only meal fit for the gods was his own son. He chopped up Pelops and served him in a sauce of ambrosia. Eat. Eat. Zeus sniffed the dinner. Demeter, the goddess who does the crops, had recently lost her daughter, Persephone, to the underworld. She absent-mindedly ate a shoulder of Pelops at the same moment Zeus recognized the menu. Zeus sent down a thunderbolt that atomized the table. Zeus sent Great Grandpa Tantalus to Hades where he lives in torment to this day beneath a fruit tree that snaps out of reach whenever he reaches for it, standing in a pool of water that evaporates down a drain the moment he kneels to drink. Talk about jokes gone bad. Zeus reassembled Pelops with a shoulder of ivory to replace the one Demeter had eaten. You with me?

C: Great-grandfather Tantalus. Son Pelops. Feast. More of Zeus' curses. Got it.

A: Pelops fell in love with the daughter of local gentry, Hippodameia—

C: Hippodameia

A: —whose very creepy father wouldn't let her go. Any man who asked to marry her received a challenge. You can marry my little girl if you can beat me in a chariot race. If the suitor lost, he was promptly murdered. Hippodameia had buried many a suitor. Pelops took the challenge. But he covered his bets. He bribed the king's charioteer to loosen the screws on the wheels of the royal chariot. The race starts. The wheel spins off. The king, tossed out, dies instantaneously. Pelops and Hippodameia get married.

C: Is that a happy ending?

A: Cassandra, we're in Greece. Yes, it is. But there's also always one thing more. The charioteer tries a little blackmail, wanting more reward for loosening the bolts on the king's chariot. Pelops meets him by a cliff and instead of paying the hush money pushes the charioteer over the cliff to his death.
As the charioteer plummets through the sky, time slows down long enough for him to curse Pelops and all his progeny to come.

C: That's you.

A: If you believe in that sort of thing. I don't. But there are days when the sky is clear I can hear that charioteer falling through space cursing the house of Tantalus.

C: Pelops and Hippodameia?

A: They had two sons. My father Atreus and my uncle Thyestes. The people of Mycenae had received advice from a local oracle that they choose their new king from among Pelops' sons. Thyestes was chosen at first, but picture this! At that moment, the sun reverses direction and sets in the east! My dad Atreus argued that because the sun reversed its path, the election of Thyestes should be reversed. The Myceneans bought that argument. Atreus became king. Thyestes was not pleased.

C: But your mother—who was she?

A: Oh god. Backtrack. Okay, back in time. We are in Crete. My mother's remarkable grandfather Minos was king of Crete. He created the world's first navy. He had the idea that a kingdom should have its own fleet of ships instead of every man for himself when trouble hit. As with so many talented men, he had a troubled family life.

C: Troubled?

A: For starters, one of his daughters, my great aunt, was Phaedra. You've heard of her?

C: I have lots of catching up to do.

A: In order to keep his throne, every nine years Minos fed seven boys and seven girls to the Minotaur who lived in the family labyrinth, again, for reasons involving oracles.

C: Minotaur?

A: You don't know who that is? A monster with the head of a bull and the body of a man?

C: You have your gods. We have ours.

A: Minos' daughter Ariadne put the whole scheme at risk. She fell for some interloper and gave him the secret to the labyrinth. He promptly slew the Minotaur and put Crete into chaos. My great-grandfather Minos left Crete on some mission involving a riddle and ended up in Sicily, being scalded to death in his bath by Daedalus, the builder of the labyrinth.

C: Oh god.

A: Minos is now in the underworld judging the dead. But it won't do me any good. I hear he doesn't play any favorites.

C: Minos. Minotaur. Phaedra. Ariadne.

A: They're only aunts. You don't have to know them.

C: But your mother?

A: Minos' son, Catreus, caught his daughter Aerope in bed with a slave and sent her off to be drowned, but a servant disobeyed and sent Aerope off to Mycenae.

C: Our destination. Where your father lived!

A: My father Atreus took one look at her and made her his. He married her!

C: Happy ending?

A: You're optimists in Troy. My father's brother, Thyestes, took a look at Aerope and raped her.

C: People don't behave like this in Troy.

A: My father played his cards well. He went to Thyestes and said, "Okay, you raped my wife but we know all evil comes from women. We're brothers. Let bygones be bygones. Come for dinner and we'll bury the hatchet."

C: I like a large, forgiving soul.

A: I hate to disappoint you. The day of the dinner my father lured his brother's boys into a trap, and, like his grandfather Tantalus before him, chopped all his nephews into bite size pieces, cooked them in a festive sauce—again the nectar of the gods being the secret ingredient—serving the children to their very own father. Gave the deceitful bastard what he deserved. This time the meal was completed. Not a crumb left. Clean plates.

C: Oh my god.

A: After Uncle Thyestes finished vomiting up his sons, he found himself so desolate, he screwed his very own daughter Pelopia, who had not been part of the feast. Together they had a son named Aegisthus.

C: Poor Pelopia!

A: It's awful what happened to Pelopia. She learned her own father was the father of her child. She killed herself. Thyestes raised Aegisthus to seek vengeance on my father and then on his sons, Menelaus and yours truly, Agamemnon. Cousin Aegisthus grew up to do as programmed. Aegisthus murdered my father.

C: Atreus.

A: Exactly, and became king of Mycenae. My brother Menelaus and I hightailed
it out of there, escaped fate, and fled to Sparta.

C: Sparta.

A: The king of Sparta had two daughters. Twin sisters, but by different fathers.
Clytemnestra was married to the king of some minor kingdom. I had to have her.
I murdered her husband. Married her. My brother married the other daughter Helen,
whose father was Zeus, and took her to Laconia where he became King
and she his queen.
I brought Clytemnestra back to Mycenae, drove Aegisthus off my father's throne with
the help of Menelaus' army, and became the man you see today, king of Mycenae.
Queen Clytemnestra and Queen Helen. Those two girls turned out all right. Menelaus
and I turned out well. Defied the fates. Soared to the heights. Skirted the curses.
Loved by the masses. Life is good.
And then my brother came to see me. A bad apple seduced my brother's wife and
abducted her to some backwater that's nowhere unless you're going
to the Dardenelles.

C: Sacred Troy! And my brother was no bad apple. He got trapped by a tart you now
tell me was fathered by a swan. That I never heard! Your tart sister-in-law found
herself married to an old man and needed some juice in her bed.

A: Let's not fight the Trojan War over again.

C: She stole a comb from me. A brooch.

A: Royals acting badly. Let's talk about royals acting royally! The magnitude!
I assembled a thousand ships. Off to Troy. Shock and awe. This will take a few days.
I'd restore Helen to my brother's bed in record time.

C: Ten years ago.

A: My only sadness back then? Our adventure couldn't start. The gods withheld
the one thing we needed. The air was dead. My advisor said the gods are suckers
for the sacrifice of a loved one. Get their attention! I loved no one more than
my daughter, Iphigenia. I needed that wind. I could always have another daughter.

C: You killed her.

A: Sacrificed! On an altar. All very proper. Not some back alley. There is a difference.

And it worked. The gods gave us the wind that blew us to Troy. And here we are.
Ten years later. Sailing home. My wife. My three girls. My boy. My people. All waiting
for the victors.

C: You set out with a thousand ships.

A: You could step from one ship to the next to reach Troy.

C: And look behind us now.

A: Don't look back!

C: I count five.

A: Look ahead. The air.

C: A thousand ships leave. Five return. It doesn't seem a victory to me.

A: It will when you see how we are greeted.

C: By strangers.

A: To you. Not to me. Your new family. You know all. You've climbed the family tree.

C: Minotaur. Crete. Aerope. Rape. Thyestes. Atreus. Agamemnon. Menelaus.
Revenge. Cannibalism. Seduction. Kidnapping. Infanticide. Hostile invasion. E-I-E-I-O.

A: You make it all sound tawdry.

C: Someone told me the gods snatched up Helen and moved her to Egypt for
the past ten years and put a double in her place.

A: Wars breed the damnedest stories. Menelaus and Helen are back in Sparta.
Finally happy ending. Breathe deep. The air.

C: Did the wind just shift?

A: You'll love my people, flush with victory.

C: Is that a storm cloud?

A: I'd prefer it if you didn't sleep with any of them.

C: Why is the sea suddenly rough?

A: The sea is excited to have us home! Wait—it is a storm—Hello? Row? Faster!

C: We'll arrive.

A: The storm blocks the coast.

C: Clytemnestra greets us.

A: Of course she will. I'll work it out with her. The sun is supposed to shine
on the victors! Please don't go into one of your trances.

C: She's planning a banquet.

A: Of course. A born hostess.

C: For you.

A: Who else?

C: All the troops on this ship.

A: All the sailors? No! A small intimate family dinner now that I'm home. Family. Orestes. Electra. Chrysothemis. You. I'll invite you. You're trying to frighten me with the future. You don't have that gift. You told me that to scare me. You're my slave. I can sell you to whomever I want.

C: Aegisthus is back in the picture.

A: Never.

C: He's in her bed.

A: Clytemnestra? Her sister Helen may have the morals of a raccoon but Clytemnestra—? There's a word. Unimpeachable. You are making trouble.

C: You killed her daughter. Perhaps she's angry.

A: Killed? Sacrifice. Blame the gods. They were the ones demanding it. No trances. Sit up.

C: A double-headed axe.

A: Clytemnestra's first husband carried a double-headed ax.

C: The one you used to kill him.

A: I freed her from him.

C: Perhaps she doesn't think of it that way.

A: Clytemnestra keep an axe? Wait till you meet her. Sit up! No trances! What is this storm? Who's steering this ship? Hello!

C: She asks all your men who've survived ten years at Troy into the royal hall for a welcome home dinner.

A: As she should.

C: The wine flows.

A: As it will.

C: Everyone is sleepy.

A: A long voyage.

C: Clytemnestra raises her hand.

A: Calling for a waiter.

C: Aegisthus and his men appear.

A: He's nowhere in the picture. I conquered him. Sent him into exile. Bested him. That's the word. He's wandering the earth.

C: Clytemnestra hands him the double-headed axe. He begins his slaughter. Clytemnestra asks to hold the axe. She slaughters you.

A: You're being very hostile.

C: They slaughter me as well.

A: Oh, and you die too? What grandiosity, inserting yourself into the picture to spoil my homecoming. You say these things to put me in a bad mood. To kill the triumph.

C: Years later. Orestes kills his mother.

A: You're trying to put terror into me. I see your plan. You don't want to arrive at Mycenae. You're trying to frighten me away, pretending you have your curse back. You want me to steer this ship to a different port, one where you have allies. You hate that I'm the victor. Killed your father. We won. You lost. You can't piss on my parade. We're going home! The future, like my fate, is for me to decide. Fate is for the little guy. The sun is out. The sea calm. The storm passed. See the coast. You'll love Mycenae.

C: I see a book.

A: A what?

C: Of photographs.

A: Of what?

C: Images of Mycenae captured by a machine. Ancient walls constructed by the Cyclops—giants from long ago—but your palace and all the houses in ruins.

A: No, that's Troy. Not Mycenae!

C: You enter up a ramp. A gate. Ten feet high, ten feet wide.

A: The gate to my city. The largest gate in the world!

C: It narrows as it reaches the top.

A: How do you know this?

C: At the top on the lintel, two stone lionesses confront each other.

A: Yes!

C: They rest on a pillar of Minoan design.

A: In honor of our forebears from Crete. Who told you these things about my home?

A book appears, suspended in mid-air. CASSANDRA gives it to AGAMEMNON.
HE turns pages.

A: This can't be Mycenae.

C: My curse is back.

A: What are these images?

C: By Robert McCabe.

A: Is he a sorcerer?

C: It's his name.

A: Who'd name anyone Robert McCabe? You lie. You want me to steer this boat to another port. A place where you have allies. You think you're being clever. You have no curse. I don't believe Apollo even cursed you! It's something you made up to give yourself power. I don't believe you.

AGAMEMNON throws the book overboard.

C: Orestes will kill his mother. Orestes will kill Aegisthus. The Furies will drive Orestes mad until Athena intervenes. Orestes will rule Mycenae until he is bitten one day by a scorpion and dies. No heirs. The house of Tantalus comes to an end.

A: We are forever! Look ahead! Land ho! Home. Let the happiness begin. Don't think anyone here will believe you and your curse. You're my slave. My souvenir. Breathe deep!

C: It's back. Thank you, Apollo. The future is here.

THE END

pp. 128–29

The southwest extremity of the Acropolis is highlighted by the sun against the still dark north face of Mount Zara.

Agamemnon Dassis with his daughter Panagoula (Loula) at the door of the Belle Helene inn. Agamemnon was one of the four sons of Dimitris Dassis, exacavation foreman for Professor Tsountas. The Homeric welcome over the door was first painted in the 1930s (and later repainted) by Peggy MacVeagh Thorne, daughter of Lincoln MacVeagh, American Minister to Greece from 1933–41. His family, who were frequent visitors to Mycenae and featured the site in their delightful children's book *Greek Journey*, gave major donations toward the building of the village church of St. Panteleimon. The text (Odyssey 1.123) reads, "Greetings stranger. You will be welcomed here by us."

As one nears the Acropolis, along the modern road, it appears silhouetted against the pass to Berbati.

ROBERT McCABE **MYCENAE**

A tourist walks up toward the Acropolis from the Treasury of Atreus to the southwest. The site appears clearly against Mount Prophet Ilias behind.

Alan Wace with the excavation architect for 1954, Herschel Sheppard, looking toward the Acropolis and Mount Prophet Ilias from beside the modern road to the west.

A passing cloud darkens Mount Prophet
Ilias behind the sunlit Acropolis, seen
here from the entry to the dromos of the
Treasury of Atreus.

Burning on the lower slopes of the Acropolis. The dry weed stubble was cleared from the site by burning at the start of each season, but a random cigarette butt could also start an unwanted fire.

pp. 140–41
From high on rugged Mount Zara—not often climbed—there is an unusual view of the Acropolis from the southeast. The newly restored terraces, which held up the Court and Megaron complex of the Palace, show starkly. Mount Kyllene, the birthplace of Hermes, can be seen in the distance to the northwest.

The distant view of the Acropolis from
the east for the traveller coming from
the northeast or from Berbati.

A closer view of the Acropolis from the
east, from the lower slopes of Mount
Prophet Ilias.

pp. 146–47
The lower slopes of Mount Prophet Ilias
to the east of the Acropolis.

Below the north side of the Acropolis, the modern tracks divide following the lines of the Mycenaean roads running northwards to the west and to the east of Mount Prophet Ilias.

The north side of the Acropolis in the early morning from the lower slopes of Mount Prophet Ilias; Mount Artemision can be seen on the horizon.

The Acropolis from the northeast seen
from somewhat higher on the slope of
Mount Prophet Ilias. The north end of
the Argive plain and the modern road to
Corinth can be seen beyond. The Mycenaean road to the southwest led directly across the plain towards Argos, passing the site at Khania on its route.

The Manos family encampment above the Acropolis, on the slopes of Mount Prophet Ilias, with a wooden cradle for the baby.

ROBERT McCABE **MYCENAE**

Christos Manos and his mother Sophia, photographed at their encampment on the slopes of Mount Prophet Ilias. The family had a long tradition as shepherds.

The approach to the Lion Gate, with the East Bastion under repair.

pp. 158–59
Restoring the East Bastion of the entrance to the Lion Gate. The simple scaffold and pulley used in the 1950s is probably very similar to that used by the original builders in the Bronze Age.

The North Bastion of the Citadel.

The Lion relief over the main gateway to the Acropolis.

pp. 164–65
The Lion Gate and its entrance passage seen from the scaffolding of the restoration work on the east wall.

Detail of the threshold of the Lion Gate. The deep channels, once thought to be wheel ruts from long usage are now considered more recent drainage channels. The crosscuts to stop slippage could be of any date.

ROBERT McCABE **MYCENAE**

The West Bastion of the entryway to the Lion Gate was built in regular courses of the local conglomerate stone; this bastion formed the defense against the unprotected sword hand of an approaching enemy.

From the top of the East Bastion of the
Lion Gate there are magnificent views
across Grave Circle A and over the Citadel
Wall to the Treasury of Atreus and the
plain of Argos, stretching beyond to the
two hills of Argos, the peaked Larissa
and the flat Aspis (shield).

Charles Williams (excavation architect 1955) sketching, sitting in the shade of the Lion Gate.

Looking in through the Lion Gate toward
the Great Ramp.

The Lion Gate and the Great Ramp from
the top of the East Bastion.

View over Grave Circle A toward the Gulf of Nauplion, with Mount Zara on the left and Argos on the right in the distance.

pp. 178–79
The west side of Grave Circle A, looking south towards the sea along the line of the ancient road that led to the Argive Heraion (Mycenaean Prosymna) and beyond.

Looking from the Great Ramp over the south side of Grave Circle A and across the Citadel Wall to the group of rich merchants' houses that flanked the side of the road approaching the Citadel from the south. Three of these buildings were excavated by the British team at this time; a fourth was discovered and excavated by the Archaeological Society of Athens when the modern road was widened for tourist buses.

Detail of the entrance to Grave Circle A
looking across the plain to Argos.

Alan Wace beside the orthostats of Grave
Circle A. The Acropolis of Argos in the
background.

View west over the south side of Grave
Circle A. This photograph appeared in
the 1955 exhibition at Princeton about
the decipherment of Linear B.

Back of the slab with the Lion relief.

pp. 190–91
The inner face of the Lion Gate and the
Acropolis wall to the west during reconstruction of the east wall of the entrance
passage. Note the rough masonry at the
base of the inner Acropolis wall at this
point, showing that this section would
not have been visible. This section is
thought to have been the site of a staircase to a walkway on top of the wall,
possibly with stables beneath.

The south side of Grave Circle A with the Great Ramp behind. Mount Prophet Ilias forms a backdrop as ever.

The Great Ramp and Grave Circle A with the as-yet-unexcavated section of the South House and the Cult Center to the south; a group of visitors views the valley from the top of the Hellenistic Tower.

From the top of the Great Ramp looking
across the House of the Warrior Vase and
the South House towards the Treasury
of Atreus and Argos.

pp. 198–199
The interior of the Lion Gate with the so-
called Granary and the entrance to Grave
Circle A. The Granary was built after the
great destruction of 1200 BC as some kind
of civic administration re-emerged. The
building was nicknamed from the finds
of wheat, barley, and vetches found there.
Mount Kyllene can be seen on the horizon.
Charles Williams is visible in the Gate.

The height of the surround slabs of the
Grave Circle can be judged from the two
tourists in the entryway, rendering impossible Schliemann's idea that this enclosure might have been some kind of
bench. Charles Williams is still at work in
the shade of the Gate.

The Grand Staircase that led to the Palace Court.

The Grand Staircase, which lay at the top
of the roadway leading from the Cult
Center to the Court of the Megaron,
viewed from above.

The southwest extremity of the Acropolis
in the afternoon light.

The southwest extremity of the Acropolis in the early morning light, silhouetted against the shadow of Mount Zara with the Argive plain beyond.

ROBERT McCABE **MYCENAE**

A striking view from the south end of
the Acropolis looking across to the Treasury of Atreus and the Panagia chapel.

ROBERT McCABE **MYCENAE**

Standing on a heavy terrace held up by the Citadel Wall on the south side of the summit lies the Megaron Complex—the heart of a Mycenaean palace structure. This doorway leads from the Porch to the Anteroom of the Megaron itself.

ROBERT McCABE **MYCENAE**

The "Throne Room" or "Guest Suite" on the summit of the Acropolis viewed from the north and looking towards the Treasury of Atreus and the Argive plain (Argos in the background)—shaded shortly after sunrise by the shadow of Mount Zara.

Detail of the base of the stair at the northwest corner of the Great Court of the Palace.

ROBERT McCABE MYCENAE

Detail of masonry in the Hellenistic polygonal style from the west of the Lion Gate. This section of the Citadel wall was demolished by the Argives in 468 BC in revenge for the participation of Mycenae at the Battle of Plataea against the Persians. The walls were later restored in the Hellenistic period.

The corbel-vaulted Sally Port, which opens onto the defensive terrace overlooking the Chavos Ravine to the south of the Acropolis, with Mount Zara behind.

View through the Sally Port.

The Postern or North Gate from the inside.

Entrance to the Secret Cistern with the original east wall of the Citadel on the left. The cistern, to which was piped water from the Perseia spring in the pass to the east, was originally outside the walls but later an extended approach through the new northeast extension wall of the Citadel gave protection to this vital supply. Much of the water used in the village (and on the site) still comes from this spring.

Staircase leading down to the main cistern, often called the Secret Cistern.

The facade of the Treasury of Atreus. A couple of years later Charles Williams was lowered from above by rope to make detailed measurements of the dowel holes and to study other traces of how the decorative blocks of red and green stone were held in place.

Detail of the cap stones of the Treasury of Atreus.

ROBERT McCABE **MYCENAE**

Alan and Helen Wace at the far end of the dromos of the Treasury of Atreus.

Looking out along the dromos of the
Treasury of Atreus from the level of the
lintel; Helen Wace scurrying to get out
of the photograph.

pp. 232–33
Alan Wace writing up the day's work in
his notebook on the Panagia Ridge. The
excavation team can be seen starting
work in the foreground with Christos
Brekos, who served as assistant to the
architect for many years, holding the
survey staff in the background. Notice-
able are the thick head scarves on two
of the older men; these were all-purpose
squares of striped homespun cloth that
could be used as aprons, cummerbunds,
head scarves, or for carrying lunch.

Alan Wace observing one of Mycenae's skilled pickmen (Dimitris Papadopoulos) opening a new trench on the slope west of the modern road, across from the House of Shields and the House of the Oil Merchant. Some of the villagers had worked for Alan Wace in the excavations of the 1920s, others were recent recruits. Many became exceptionally skilled with the small pick (*skalistiri*).

Looking northeast across the dromos of the Tomb of Clytemnestra. Seats of the Hellenistic theater are visible in the foreground and excavation of the Poros Wall, which capped the outside of the tomb, can be seen on the other side of the dromos.

Tourists visit the Tomb of Clytemnestra,
where the roof damaged by Veli Pasha
in the early nineteenth century had recently been restored.

Lisa Wace French and Charles Williams
wait for this photograph to be taken
from inside the Tomb of the Genii (sometimes called the Perfect Tomb for its
excellent state of preservation).

The seats of the Hellenistic theater over the dromos of the Tomb of Clytemnestra.

pp. 244–45
Looking southwest across the dromos of the Tomb of Clytemnestra. The seats of the Hellenistic theater can be seen in the foreground on the left and in the background one can see the excavation of the House of Shields.

Cleaning a Hellenistic grave on the slope
outside the Lion Gate.

Lisa Wace French and a fraction of Charles Williams at the Cyclopean Tomb.

pp. 250–51

Alan Wace on an excursion to find the Palace of Menelaus. Here he looks out across the plain near Sparta, where he had been a member of the excavation team from the British School from 1906 to 1910. They worked on the Classical/Roman site and on the Sanctuary of Artemis Orthia. A small excavation was carried out on the Menelaion hill as well. There a Mycenaean mansion complex was found, but it seemed small and ill-suited to be the Bronze Age Palace of Menelaus—a site that has been much sought over the last century. Now the remains recently discovered at Agios Vasileios near the Tholos Tomb of Vaphio, where tablets in the Linear B script have been found, seem to fulfill all the criteria.

Alan Wace sherding near Sparta. Wace and Carl Blegen always used the term "oxyderking" for this exercise of walking over a site with the eyes keenly focused on the ground for sherds or any other traces of occupation. The term was based on the Homeric Greek epithet ὀξυδερκής (oxyderkes) meaning "sharp-eyed".

ROBERT McCABE **MYCENAE**

The Waces on a hill across the Eurotas River from Sparta, where the later shrine of Menelaos and Helen is situated. Wace (under the directorship of Dawkins) had excavated a Mycenaean building here in 1910. He had always hoped to do further work on the site; the excavation was continued by Hector Catling in the 1980s.

The old sign at the turnoff for Mycenaean Pylos, the Palace of Nestor, which lies on the far southwest coast of the Peloponnese. This site was excavated by Professor Carl Blegen of the American School of Classical Studies at Athens, who had worked at Mycenae in 1920 with Alan Wace and identified the new site. This was thanks to material on the surface, which Blegen recognized from his work at Mycenae as being the burnt debris from an important structure. It was at Pylos that a large cache of Linear B tablets was discovered.

Repairing the excavation jeep in Argos.
Jeeps left behind by the military became
useful all-purpose excavation vehicles
—that of Carl Blegen at Pylos was even
found to have a live hand grenade under
the driver's seat. Argos was the local
market town where anything and
everything would be sought and usually obtained. The mechanics were particularly good. Large trucks like that in
the photo were used to convey overnight
fruit and vegetables from the rich gardens
of the Argolid to the markets of Athens.
Often trucks formed part of the dowry
given with a young bride to enable her
husband to set himself up in business.

Beside the kitchen block behind the Hotel Belle Helene with Agamemnon Dassis in a cook's apron at the door and his wife Vassiliki (Vasso) doing laundry. The deckchairs of Alan Wace's excavation team can be seen under the trees in the front yard. Orestes, a younger brother, was the usual cook but he also served as excavation foreman. The side of the original front section of the inn can be seen; this was later destroyed to build the current large front reception area needed to cater to the bus tours that visit the site.

Above the village on the north Dimitri Georgitsopoulos and his young son Sotirios (with Theodosios Tsenos behind) stand beside the enclosure of branches (*kladia*) where they will plant tobacco seeds and grow the seedlings to be planted out in the fields. On the rock outcrop behind is a quarry of the conglomerate stone from which much of the handsome building on the Citadel was constructed.

Making mud bricks just outside the modern village.

Evening on the terraces northwest of
the Citadel on the lower slopes of the
Pezoulia area: a villager sitting sidesaddle on his donkey leads in the horses.

The small church of St. George by the village cemetery, now rebuilt and enlarged thanks to the growing wealth of the village. This cemetery holds the graves of George Mylonas and his wife Lela, and of Humfry Payne (Director of the British School and excavator of Perachora).

The beach which stretches along the coast of the bay east of Asine towards the little market town of Drepanon. This was a favorite weekend haunt for generations of British archaeologists working on the finds from Mycenae in the museum at Nauplion. We called it "Stony Tolo" to differentiate it from the beautifully sandy, child-friendly but dull beach of the town of Tolo itself.

pp. 270–71
Moonlight effect through the backs of the upper blocks of the Lion Gate.

DANIEL FALLU

THE MYCENAEAN LANDSCAPE
FROM "WELL-FOUNDED" TO A SHAKY END

When one reads Homer's *Iliad* and *Odyssey*, the clear protagonists are the kings of the Achaean kingdoms: Agamemnon, Menelaus, Nestor, and Achilles, among others. The exploits of these kings and generals fill the epics, while the landscape serves as a backdrop, cruel and unforgiving to soldiers of the *Iliad*, or fantastical and exotic for the sailors of the *Odyssey*. In fact, Homer saw little point in including any description of Mycenae's natural surroundings, focusing instead on the "well-built" citadel and its royal family. This landscape, however, was and is just as dynamic, and perhaps as vengeful, as Achilles and his ilk: it shaped the story of the Mycenaeans and was in turn shaped by them. While even ancient civilizations were not at the complete mercy of the natural environment, the dynamic geological and environmental backdrop of Mycenae certainly played a part in the prosperity and subsequent collapse of the Palace of Agamemnon.

WELL-FOUNDED MYCENAE

Although "Golden Mycenae" is probably best remembered for its wealth and burials, Homer's description of "Well-built," or "Well-founded Mycenae" is equally apt: the ancient citadel was strengthened not only by the stone in its walls but by the rugged rock of the surrounding hills and mountains. The acropolis hill of Mycenae is a small limestone hill rising before a pass between the Charvati and Zara mountains. This positioning allowed Mycenae control over and access to farmland in the Berbati Valley, and through the pass northwards to Nemea and Corinth. The steep slope of the mountains and the receding plain generated deeply incised ravines, namely the Kokoretsa Ravine to the north and the Chavos to the southeast.

Aside from providing a natural defense, and restricting access essentially to two roads from the northeast and the southwest (Jansen 1998), these two ravines mark two dif-

Looking west along the Chavos Ravine, which runs to the south of the Acropolis toward the Treasury of Atreus on the hill slope opposite.

ferent landscapes: to the north, a series of torrential streams cut through soft, younger rocks generating small ravines and fertile tracts of land. To the south, the Chavos Ravine passes along the boundary between these softer rocks and hard, old limestones creating a narrow flood plain subject to frequent landslides from the slopes of Mount Zara (Higgins and Higgins 1996). Although both of these landscapes are equally fertile, and today support the full range of fruit trees, vines, and olive trees that are the agricultural staples of the region, the incised valleys and the gentle slopes to the north are less prone to sudden erosion, and therefore preferable for agriculture (Zangger 1992). Indeed the arrangement of the fifteen known Bronze Age cemeteries to the north and west of the citadel, containing a sum of over 250 tombs, would suggest that much of the Mycenaeans' attention was focused on this stable soil (Jansen 1998).

Although Mycenae's access to agricultural land, whether its own holdings or those of its ally Tiryns in the Argive Plain, is indisputable, access to water is a more complicated issue. Streams in the Argolid are unreliable sources of water, only flowing during heavy winter rains, while the nearest "standing water" was marshland known as Lake Lerna, legendary home of the multi-headed Hydra, seventeen kilometers away. Channels through the bedrock, caused by the corrosive rainwater and contacts between rock layers of varying hardness, cause frequent and more perennial springs which well up along the bases of mountains or smaller rock outcrops such as those rocky hills on which Mycenae, Tiryns, and Midea were founded. The Perseia spring, which rises from soft, younger geological deposits in the pass between Zara and Charvati, may play a role in the mythology of Mycenae's heroic founding, as it is said that Perseus stopped by a spring where mushrooms, μύκης (mykes) grew. Today, this spring waters a large oak tree which provides shade to goats and goatherds.

The spring was harnessed in the second millennium BC to feed the "secret cistern" carved fifteen meters deep into the bedrock of the acropolis, while a separate aqueduct led eastward, possibly feeding agricultural fields. Before this, inhabitants of the citadel most likely relied on wells, such as that found on the north slope of the acropolis at

Petsas House. A possible reservoir, created by the damming of the lower Chavos channel in the area of the modern Church of St. George, has been hypothesized but not yet proven (Palaiologou 2014). While it is clear from the existence and momentary success of the site that the Mycenaeans found a way to adapt to the potential water deficit, this high-altitude environment would not always sustain a rich and thriving community, and the landscape that permitted settlement and prosperity would have its part to play in the collapse of Mycenae.

CHANGE AND COLLAPSE

Just as society and geology interacted to give Mycenae an advantage, so too would the natural environment that once supported them contribute to its downfall. Around 1200 BC, the palaces of Bronze Age Greece ceased to function, buildings were destroyed by fire, and walls tumbled apparently by earthquakes. What followed did not resemble the palatial Mycenaean culture: monumental buildings, record-keeping, and the precious artifacts that characterized the Mycenaean elites disappeared and did not return for several centuries (French 1996).

The Chavos Ravine, which played its part in sheltering an infant Mycenae, may have also had a hand in the sudden events of the twelfth century BC. The Argolid, wherein lie Mycenae, Tiryns, and Midea, is an active seismic zone, being ringed by substantial faults in the bedrock (Maroukian et al. 1996). The instability of the bedrock beneath the ancient citadel is highlighted by a long exposed fault running east to west along the northern boundary of the citadel and the northern slope of Mount Zara. Successive earthquakes, which caused the fault to slip approximately one –and–a–half meters, resulted in the redirection of the Chavos stream, cutting off the water supply to the ravine and the terraces south of the acropolis (Maroukian et al. 1996). The site continued to be used through the worst of the damage, although the Cult Center, previously a large complex of shrines and altar spaces, was reused after the earthquakes, probably as a residential complex (French 1996). Around this time, Mycenaean remains downstream from the citadel were buried under more than two meters of soil eroded from Mount Zara. This same soil, the result of a short series of large-scale erosional events on mountain slopes, is mirrored by two similar events that occurred at the nearby site of Chania, only three kilometers away but receiving sediments from a different set of mountains. These landslides occurred a century after Tiryns in the Argive Plain was first buried by "floods" coming from the nearby hills.

Chief among the "usual suspects" for the Mycenaean Collapse is drought, bringing with it economic hardship and civil strife. In his *Meteorologica*, written in 350 BC, Aristotle is perhaps the first to voice this theory:

> In the time of the Trojan wars the Argive land was marshy and could only support a small population, whereas the land of Mycenae was in good condition (and for this reason Mycenae was the superior). But now the opposite is the case, for the reason we have mentioned: the land of Mycenae has become completely dry and barren, while the Argive land that was formerly barren owing to the water has now become fruitful. Now the same process that has taken place in this small district must be supposed to be going on over whole countries and on a large scale.

Located higher in the mountains, Mycenae would indeed have had the potential for drought, as ground water would be scarcer and storm clouds would often be "rained out" by their passage over the surrounding mountains creating a "rain shadow" in the northern reaches of the Argolid. A shift in the prevailing winds could effectively drive Mycenae to thirst, a phenomenon that has occurred in recent history (Carpenter 1969, Bryson et al. 1974, Zerefos and Zerefos 1978). This pattern of suddenly drier conditions may have occurred elsewhere in the eastern Mediterranean after 1200 BC, but there is no evidence of a sudden drought at this time in Greece. Instead, a long period of increasingly drier climate punctuated by intense rainfall is likely, reaching its peak in the Early Iron Age, centuries after the palaces fell (Drake 2012).

This drying trend may have prevailed for most of the reign of the Mycenaean palaces, from 1600 BC on into the Early Iron Age, popularly known as the "Greek Dark Ages." A closer look at Mycenaean civilization may show us that this civilization "made its career" in adapting to an increasingly hostile natural environment. Agricultural terracing was introduced to Greece during the Bronze Age, with an increase in use supposed for the Late Bronze Age. At Gla, in Boeotia, a substantial tract of seasonal marshland was drained using a system of natural sinkholes and artificial canals (Iakovidis 1998). Only at the end of the Bronze Age, and in the Argolid district specifically, did the environmental situation become dire. At Tiryns, only seventeen kilometers from Mycenae, a massive earthen-bank dam was constructed in order to redirect flood waters that resulted in the burial of the Mycenaean town outside the fortification walls of the citadel (Zangger 1994). This flood, and landslides at the site of Mycenae at Chania (Palaiologou 2014), may have similar causes, probably being the result of isolated heavy rainstorms on parched, dry soil devoid of protective ground cover during the Late Bronze Age.

While the relationship between climate, earthquakes, and the demise of the palace of Mycenae is "shaky" at best, we can say for certain that the landscape around the famous citadel had a substantial influence on both its founding and its destruction. There is no doubt that, regardless of what happened elsewhere during the final centuries of the Bronze Age, the Argolid was victim to a complex interaction of increasing environmental concerns and seismic destruction, in addition to the civil strife often proposed for this era. The same bedrock that provided water and protection to the site proved, in the end, to be unreliable. Whatever happened at Mycenae the effects would seem to have been worse there than at Tiryns, which suffered similar hardship but was rebuilt in the wake of the fall of the palaces and supported a sizable town after the palatial destruction. Mycenae would go on to become a city-state in the Archaic period, four centuries later, but would never regain the prestige or control enjoyed during the days of "Golden Mycenae."

WORKS CITED

Bryson, R. A., H. H. Lamb, and D. R. Doley. "Drought and the Decline of Mycenae." *Antiquity* 48 (1974): 46–50.

Butzer, K. "Environmental History in the Mediterranean World: Cross-disciplinary Investigation of Cause-and-effect for Degradation and Soil Erosion." *Journal of Archaeological Science* 32 (2005): 1773–800.

Carpenter, R. *Discontinuity in Greek Civilization*. Cambridge: Cambridge University Press, 1966.

French, Elizabeth B. "Evidence for an Earthquake in Mycenae." In *Archaeoseismology*, edited by S.B. Stiros and R.E. Jones, 51–54. Fitch Laboratory Occasional Paper 7, Athens: Institute of Geology and Mineral Exploration and the British School at Athens, 1996.

Higgins, M. D. and R. Higgins. *A Geological Companion to Greece and the Aegean*. London: Gerald Duckworth, 1996.

Iakovidis, S. E. "Gla, Orchomène, et l'assèchement mycénien du Kopaïs." *Atti dell'Accademia Nazionale Dei Lincei, Classe Di Morali, Storiche e Filogiche: Rendiconti* 9, no. 2 (1998): 281–308.

Iakovidis, S. E. and E. French. *Archaeological Atlas of Mycenae*. Athens: The Archaeological Society of Athens, 2003.

Jansen, Anton. *A Study of the Remains of Mycenaean Roads and Stations of Bronze Age Greece*. Lewiston, New York: Edwin Mellen Press, 2002.

Maroukian, H. "Geomorphic-seismotectonic Observations in Relation to the Catastrophes at Mycenae." In *Archaeoseismology*, edited by S.B. Stiros and R.E. Jones, 189–94. Fitch Laboratory Occasional Paper 7, Athens: Institute of Geology and Mineral Exploration and the British School at Athens, 1996.

Palaiologou, H. "Water Management, Climatic, Social Changes and Agriculture in the Plain of Mycenae during the 13th C. B.C. and Later". In *Physis: L'environnement naturel et la relation homme-milieu dans le monde égéen protohistorique*, Proceedings of the 14e Rencontre égéenne internationale (Paris, 11-14 December 2012), edited by G. Touchais, R. Laffineur, and F. Rougemont, 517-520. *Aegaeum*, 37, Leuven: Peeters, 2014.

Zangger, E. "Landscape Changes around Tiryns during the Bronze Age." *American Journal of Archaeology* 98, no. 2 (1994): 189–212.

Zangger, E. "Prehistoric and Historic Soils in Greece: Assessing the Natural Resources for Agriculture." *In Agriculture in Ancient Greece*, edited by B. Wells, 13–19. (Stockholm: Swedish Institute at Athens, 1992).

Zerefos, C. S. and E. C. Zerefos. "Climatic Change in Mycenaean Greece: A Citation to Aristotle." *Archiv fur Meteorologie Geophysik und Bioklimatologie* (1978): 297–303.

ACKNOWLEDGMENTS

We are deeply grateful for the generous help of the academician and General Secretary of the Archaeological Society, Vasileios Petrakos, and of professor Nagia Polychronacou Sgouritsa, as well as archaeologist and author Christos Boulotis. They suggested bibliography, clarified many points, checked terminology, and corrected misconceptions and mistakes. We sincerely thank them.

We warmly thank the 4th Ephorate of Prehistoric and Classical Antiquities for their support of this project.

We are deeply grateful to Lisa Wace French for her lively and informative commentaries on the photographs—from the unique perspective of someone who has lived and worked at Mycenae for most of her life, and who has been a participant in the great adventure of bringing the Bronze Age into history. We further thank her for taking charge of the Timeline, a courageous step in a world of uncertain and moving dates. We thank Marianne McDonald for her support from the very start of this project when she identified and translated every reference to Mycenae in every extant Greek drama. We are grateful to Anna Tsokanis for her work in collecting a plethora of other important texts relating to Mycenae in literature, travel, and archaeology.

A huge thank you to Alexis Veroucas and Vassiliki Carmiri for their fresh, modern, and original design. To George Marinos and Sophie Panou deep thanks for their fine work and their patience in the preparation of the photographs. To Professor Kim Shelton of Berkeley—and Mycenae—profound gratitude for sharing her unique knowledge and perspective on the people and the place. Thanks to Massimo Tonolli and his team at Trifolio for their extraordinary skill in printing photographs in tritone.

We wish to convey our deepest appreciation to the National Library of Scotland for allowing us to reproduce their beautiful and historic manuscript map of Mycenae drawn by Vassilios Drosinos of Nauplion for his remarkable client, Mr. Heinrich Schliemann. We thank the Archaeological Society of Athens and Lisa Wace French for permission to use the up-to-date map of the excavated areas of the Citadel, based on a map by Spyros Iakovidis. We thank the Packard Humanities Institute for permission to print Simone Pomardi's beautiful drawing of the facade of the Treasury of Atreus.

We thank the National Archaeological Museum in Athens for permission to publish photographs of some of the extraordinary objects in their Mycenaean collection and for their help in identifying individual photographs. We want to especially thank the staff of the Photographic Archives, and Dr. George Kavvadias and Maria Chidiroglou, as well as the photographers Kostas Xenakakis, Giannis Patrikianos, and E.A. Galanopoulos.

Our deep thanks to Anna Pataki for her unwavering support for this project. We thank Ifigeneia Tournaviti for her help in translating the original Greek into English, and Andrea Schroth for her assistance in translating and proofreading.

We are immensely pleased to welcome our new collaborators in the Abbeville edition of the book, namely John Guare, Daniel Fallu, Chris Kaeser, Titina Chalmatzi, and Sophia Gani. We thank them for their enthusiasm and creativity.

We warmly thank the following for their help and support: James Ottaway Jr., Jim Wright, Marie Mauzy, Dimitri Stefanou, Michael Cosmopoulos, John Younger, Andy Szegedy-Maszak, Natalia Vogeikoff, Jack Davis, Takis Karkanas, and Anne McCabe. We thank Bob Abrams and Shannon Connors at Abbeville for their invaluable contributions in shaping the U.S. Edition.

Athina Cacouri
Robert McCabe

Editor: Shannon Connors
Production manager: Louise Kurtz
Designers: Alexis Veroucas & Vassiliki Carmiri
Map: Christopher Kaeser
Portraits: Titina Chalmatzi
Timeline: Lisa Wace French
Scans from the negatives: George Marinos and Sophie Panou
Printing and binding: Trifolio Srl, Verona, Italy

First published in the United States of America in 2016 by Abbeville Press, 116 West 23rd Street, New York, NY 10011

A version of this book was first published in Greece in 2014 by Patakis Publishers, Panagis Tsaldari (former Piraeus) 38, 104 37, Athens, Greece

First edition
10 9 8 7 6 5 4 3 2 1

ISBN 978-0-7892-1254-2

Library of Congress Cataloging-in-Publication Data available upon request.

For bulk and premium sales and for text adoption procedures, write to Customer Service Manager, Abbeville Press, 116 West 23rd Street, New York, NY 10011, or call 1-800-ARTBOOK (U.S. only).

Visit Abbeville Press online at www.abbeville.com.

Robert A. McCabe's website is www.mccabephotos.com.

6/24

ADRIATIC
SEA

IONIAN
SEA

DELPHI

ITHACA

CORINTH

MYCENAE

SPARTA

PYLOS

MEDITERRANEAN SEA

NEMEA

5 miles

5 km

MYCENAE

ARGOS

TIRYNS

ASINE

LERNA

ARGOLIC
GULF

100 miles

100 km